HOW TO GET THE JOB YOU WANT IN 30 DAYS

Wendy Stehling Drumm &
Larry E. Drumm

LONGMEADOW
P R E S S

Copyright © 1992 by Larry E. Drumm

Published by Longmeadow Press
201 High Ridge Road, Stamford, CT 06904

All rights reserved. No part of this book may be repro-
duced or utilized in any form or by any means, electronic
or mechanical, including photocopying, recording or by
any information storage and retrieval system, without
permission in writing from the Publisher.

Cover design by Jonette Jakobson

Interior design by Richard Oriolo

The author and publisher make no warranties, either
expressed or implied, with respect to the advice or information contained in this book. The author and publisher
shall not be liable for any damages arising out of the use
of the materials contained herein.

Library of Congress Cataloging-in-Publication Data

Drumm, Wendy Stehling.
How to get the job you want in 30 days: the book that
puts you back to work!
/by Wendy Stehling Drumm & Larry Drumm. — 1st ed.
p. cm.
1. Job hunting. I. Drumm, Larry, II. Title.
HF5383.D78   1992
650. 14—dc20   92-14069
                                                CIP

ISBN 0-681-41698-X

PRINTED IN THE UNITED STATES OF AMERICA

First Edition

0 9 8 7 6 5 4 3 2 1

To Larry.
I Love You.
(that's an understatement!)

An acknowledgment to our readers.
This is one of the hardest times in your life.

We pray this book helps.

CONTENTS

GOOD MORNING!

That's the way every day in the next 30 days begins for *you*, because this book is putting *you* to work. Now!

Look, no fancy introductions. You're out of work, we've been out of work, everyone near and dear to us has looked for work.

It's a drag.

It doesn't matter if you're a chairman of the board and have been kicked off your own board or if you're a tap dancer on a cruise ship that just got put in dry dock—you're facing the same dilemma:

I WANT A JOB AND I WANT IT NOW!

So we're going to help you find one. With our guidance, support, and encouragement you are going to *do*, over and over, day after exciting day, what it takes to find a job.

There are lots of great books that tell you how to do a résumé, how to interview, but this book is going to take you on a different mission.

You are going into the Hidden Job Market. You are going to penetrate to where 80 percent or more of the jobs exist. That's what U.S. Labor Department statistics say, and more important, that's what all job hunters find out!

You are going in *prepared* and *articulate, ready* and *armed* with knowledge to win the job that hundreds, even thousands, of people competing with you will *never even know about!*

You'll experience and use Referent Power. You'll stick with a Thirty-Day Action Plan that gets you to do everything you know you *should* be doing to reach your Number-One Job Goal.

So what are you waiting for?

Turn the page and GET THAT JOB!

PREPARING YOU

Review the feelings and factors
that make you unique

Assess yourself to determine your
Number-One Job Goal

Gain the knowledge needed
to prepare for networking

Get a First-Class Ticket into
the Hidden Job Market

CHAPTER 1

So How Are You Today?

"Fine."

"Come on, you're among friends. How are you *really* doing?"

"Okay."

"*How* okay?"

"Pretty okay."

"Still mad about losing your job?"

"Yeah, real !! ☉★ ◊ *! mad."

"I understand."

"No, you don't. You didn't put in fifteen years in a

company—*your whole life*—only to be kicked out with six months' pay and a crummy "retirement plan." I have a family and I'm out of work, with hardly any savings."

"How does that make you feel?"

"Scared."

"What scares you the most?"

"Not finding a job."

"Why do you think you'll have trouble finding a job?"

"I just know I will."

"Have you told anyone outside of your family that you've lost your job?"

"Nope. Just you—you're the first."

"You've come to the right place. Let's talk some more."

Right now, you may be dealing with emotions— anger, fear, betrayal, injury. *Any* feelings you have are valid and *important*. The task will be to turn all the intense negative energy you have into *positive* power.

Let's begin with your feelings of self-worth. You're probably using being out of work as a yardstick to measure your character and your stature with your family and friends. But your loved ones don't value you for your occupation, and more important, people you will be calling on for work don't use that yardstick because *they* have been out of work too. *Everybody* has gone through some job-change bad dream. Lee Iacocca got dumped from Ford! He's now one of the most admired executives in the world. You know many stories of good productive people who are out of work. Today more than ever, people find themselves out of work and it's not because of poor performance!

But back to *you*.

You're concerned about what other people think. You're turning inside yourself. You will do that for a while, but it will pass. You will talk about your anger and push your fear aside. You *will*. You have to.

The only person who can help you is you. If weeks go by and you can't get your head off the pillow, so to speak, get professional help from a psychological counselor. Seeking help is not a sign of weakness; it's a sign you want to get on with life.

The *good* news is that you bought this book. The fact that you bought it shows you want to go back to work; you *want* to help yourself.

It's very important during your unemployment that you seek out friends and relatives. Share war stories with other people out of work. Entertain, have the neighbors in, party. The more comfortable you are with yourself, the more confidence you will have in yourself.

Confidence will give you energy and power for a successful job hunt. Using the Thirty-Day Action Plan will put you into circulation. It will have you candidly admitting that you don't have a job, and, hey, you'll learn to accept that.

People aren't going to hire people who can't overcome the trauma of being out of work. They want warriors who can handle the demands of a new job. They can smell any residual anger right over the phone.

It's okay to be scared, mad, and nervous. It's *not* okay if you don't face up to taking positive action and gain control.

People who have never lost a job *do not understand* what it is like to lose a job. But there are a lot of people out there (more and more each day) who *are* losing their jobs, and they will never forget what it's like. These are the people you can gain support from by sharing feelings and stories and who can act as conduits for a job. This does not negate the help you can receive from coworkers who are still working and from your family.

The process of finding a job will continue to have its

ups and downs, and unfortunately, this book can't protect you from that. You may have already experienced the difficulty of trying to be exactly what one want ad describes one day and what another want ad describes the next day. In order to find a job, you may have tried to be a chameleon that changes with every job description. This undermines your confidence, confuses your goals, and adds to the frustrations of finding the job you want.

One of the hardest things to deal with is the lack of money you may be experiencing. It becomes particularly difficult when the time comes to buy gifts for the ones you love and you realize that it is your being out of work that prevents you from giving gifts as you have in the past. Share these feelings with your loved ones; you may be surprised at the support they give you.

Back to job hunting. It will be very difficult for you to pick up the phone for the very first time and tell one of your friends that you're out of work and that you need some help. Telling the same thing to strangers isn't any easier. And when you meet people face to face in information meetings (more about these later), you will have to project an air of self-confidence and determination to get the job you want, *without* letting the cracks show.

You will find a job. Whoever you are—from A to Z, astronaut to zookeeper—you will find the work that you *want*.

What you have to look forward to with this book is the wonderful emotional high of hearing from other people who *see* you are valuable, of landing a fantastic interview, and the satisfaction of getting your first offer.

And yes, one day soon in your new job, you'll pick up the phone and be rewarded with the caller saying, "I'm out of work. Would you be so kind as to give me some advice? I was referred to you by the president of . . ."

CHAPTER 2

Factors That You Can't Control (Sort Of)

Economic

Everyone knows it is easier to find work in an expanding economy. More jobs are created, there are fewer company failures, and fewer cost-saving measures are undertaken. You yourself are now probably conserving your own cash to weather being out of work, and you and all the many others in your situation won't be turning the economy around with this spending plan.

Still, even in a shrinking economy there are sectors

of high growth. Most recently, biotechnology, health care, environmental, and pharmaceutical industry segments are growing much faster than other segments. Look for these pockets of growth. If you have experience in a growth area, you are lucky: your chances of finding employment are higher. If not, you might want to consider changing your industry segment into one that looks better in the long term. Also, even in declining segments, companies are looking to upgrade the quality of their remaining work force. So if you have special skills, are known by many companies, or are employed by the industry leader, you might find that companies who are reducing staff are good targets. Often there is backfill, where a few people are hired because the cuts were too deep or the cuts were made intentionally to open some key spots.

Political

It is a common practice for jobs to change because of political appointment. Also, governmental and world affairs can change an industry overnight. The defense industry is a good example. If you have good government contacts and know the political system, it may help you to know that many companies are always looking for people who can help them interact with the government.

Many of the workers in the defense industry have skills that can translate to other high-technology industries—electronic assembly, welding, metal working, construction, and others. The government has a way of creating job opportunities as well as destroying them. There are many governmental sites that need clean-up. Larger environmental remediation projects are looming out there. It turns out that the very sites that created defense materials now have big pollution problems, and it will be the Defense Department's job to clean them up. Look for opportunities by adapting.

Industry

Many industries are on the decline. Banking is a prime example, with well over 200,000 jobs expected to be permanently lost. But financial skills are required in every business, and the need for financing does not decrease with the number of institutions that supply it. Think how valuable your skills might be to some company that needs to raise capital. There are many other financial institutions being created by companies—for instance, GE Credit, and General Motors Financing. So look for niches in your industry. Look for suppliers or customers who might use your skills. Move from a plastics company to a plastics processor, or from a paper maker to a paper chemical company that supplies the paper maker.

Timing

Probably the single hardest factor to deal with. What if the job you are after is not going to open up for another five months, or your Number-One Job Goal was just filled at the company you wanted to join? How can you convince someone to fill or create a position sooner—that is, on *your* schedule, not theirs? You can't. You can, however, increase your number of contacts, which would increase the possibility of finding an opening sooner. With the Thirty-Day Action Plan, you can be ahead of others by being there before or as the job forms.

Bias

Age, sex, religion, ethnic background, and health. This subject is really beyond the scope of this book. But here too, as in the rest of this book, you will find that there are specialized networks of people to support you. Usually, the larger the metropolitan area, the easier it is to find local or regional chapters of specialized networks and support groups. Know your rights. Know your resources. Know your networks.

Education

Overcoming educational requirements is a particular problem when answering ads and talking with recruiters or human relations departments. Why? People who screen résumés are going to use any possible reason to screen you and others out. This is a big one. So what do you do?

Experience and, to some extent, personal chemistry can overcome some "requirements" if you are networking. After all, the job specifications may not be set yet, and that means you may be able to have them set to fit you. Educational courses you took in your career to date can also be helpful. You could do volunteer work in the areas where you are weak, which would shape up your résumé. For example, let's say you are particularly weak in accounting/financial skills. You could be a treasurer for your church or an association. You would then develop enough familiarity with the methods, jargon, and basic skills of accounting to be at ease with the subject and project a confident image.

A Final Note

No one can predict the timing of success in finding a job. It is dependent on so many factors. This book can prepare you, help you take control, and provide you with a plan that should be ultimately successful because it places the odds on your side.

CHAPTER 3

Leaving the Job You Have

The basic principles of this book still apply. Keep good notes and files, and follow up. Use Referent Power (see Chapter 10). Head for the Hidden Job Market.

Let's look at your situation right now. As long as your job isn't threatened (lucky you!), you can spread out the thirty days to a more manageable working goal, since you have to work all day too. Whatever you do, don't send out signals. Don't be late in the morning, or be sloppy, or gossip, or waste time complaining. If you are a CEO, now is not the time to have a chat with the *Wall Street Journal!* Try to stay off "60 Minutes"!

Work extra hard to keep your job.

Changing careers? Find out what skills are required. What will your new bosses be looking for?

On your résumé you will either build on your current skills or point to skills that will be important in your new job.

Let's look at a nurse. She wants to move out of hospital care. A job as a health insurance administrator looks interesting. She can point to skills that relate to her new Number-One Job Goal! She can point to her supervisory skills on the hospital floor. She can manage people. She understands costs and knows appropriate therapies. She's good with people.

The insurance companies will ask her, "Do you really want to give up on caring for patients? Do you want to drop the hands-on caring experience for a day filled with actuary meetings?"

Well, our nurse felt actuary meetings were pretty interesting, and her value-added experience made her an excellent choice for her potential employers.

So be organized about how to expand and diversify yourself. You will be asked many questions when it comes to your career change.

You have to make your contact list. Do your research. Get Referent Power and enter the Hidden Job Market. And you need to meet a goal every day. Use your advantages:

- You have an income.
- Employers will perceive you as more valuable (dumb, but true, fact of life).
- You can network through suppliers and customers without telling anyone you are looking.
- You are feeling positive.

Do your correspondence at night at home. Set up a home office. Use your lunch hour each day not to eat (unless it is with a good contact!) but to research for your next job. Call your network when you can—very early, very late.

Squeeze in your job hunting without getting caught. Pretty obvious, but I can't warn you enough that in *any* size company, people can *smell* someone on the way out. Rumors start, your behavior perpetuates the rumors, and *hasta la vista*, baby!

Be sure you do everything to follow the Thirty-Day Action Plan with every second of your spare time, but discreetly.

CHAPTER 4

Finding Your First Job

Your dilemma is unique. We want people with experience. We want to pay them entry-level pay. You want an entry-level job? Where's your experience? No job, no experience! No experience, no job!

Even if employers don't want experience, they want to:

- reduce risk of hiring an unknown
- have confidence you can do the job
- make an investment in training *only* if they feel

sure you will make an investment in staying and becoming productive

Now, with employment so tentative, with so little job security, how do you commit to them for the long term when they don't commit to you?

How do you plan for and create experience when you are so young (or you have been out of the job market and want to enter it)?

First, if you know you are going to be looking for a job in a couple of years, now is the time to begin your experience campaign. Right now you can:

- do a summer internship program
- volunteer for work in a nonprofit agency
- train yourself for special skills by looking ahead to what employers want and finding a way to get it

Also, your background might show some leadership skills, such as:

- class officer
- Eagle Scout
- a job while you are at school
- helping to pay for your own schooling
- co-op work
- summer employment

You must do exactly what the book outlines. Assess your strengths, decide your Number-One Job Goal, decide your strategy using two criteria and get into the Hidden Job Market, and build your initial list of a hundred contacts.

A hundred contacts. You've got to be kidding, right? No, we're not!! How can you, a lowly student, do that?

Well, here are the places:

- school—teachers, professors, friends (their parents)

- church or religious affiliation—clergy, other members
- people you babysat for, or whose lawns you mowed
- your volunteer work contacts
- political party—become active
- your neighbors
- your contacts in Scouts, adult leaders
- your hair stylist, postman
- fraternities, sororities

The list is endless. You may feel self-conscious about asking, but it's your future, so forget the embarrassment. (Would you rather be unemployed or embarrassed? No contest!)

Probably your most powerful tool is older people. I know it's not cool, but it works. Everyone wants to help a young person. Everyone who's older loves to give advice (you know that). This time, take the time to listen. More important, take the time to ask. Get their help with your résumé. Have them give you contacts. Use their Referent Power. It is the *strongest* weapon you have to crack the Hidden Job Market.

Older people are going to hire you and older people trust older people. You *cannot* overuse this. Now is the time for your maturity to pay off. Now is the time to grow up. Now is the time to network using older people.

MBAs are a glut, as of this writing. They are flooding the market. You have had two more years than they have had, minimum, to network and build your skills. Hope you didn't waste them. Being a walking, talking textbook won't differentiate you—employers want real-world training. Get it through volunteering, be it political parties, associations, social clubs, or nonprofit agencies. There are thousands of places that need and welcome volunteers. At the same time you are building your experience, build your network!

A Last Note

You are particularly subject to ups and downs because your ego is still developing. Find safe outlets for your feelings. In front of contacts is not the place to let your feelings out. Gatekeepers (read Chapter 6) want mature people, not whiners! Build your confidence; let it show!! Go get that job!

CHAPTER 5

Determining Your Number-One Job Goal

The more you know about what you want, the more effective you will be in getting the job you want—in thirty days.

Please take a second even if you know exactly what your job goal is and read this chapter.

It's all about making you *happy*. It's all about making you the number-one candidate of choice for a great job. You will not settle for less.

If you do not understand yourself—your shortcomings, the things you like, the type of job atmosphere you want, the way you come across to other people, and your desired salary range—you will not get the job you want. But if you know your job goal, are dedicated to getting that job, and project the energy you will have in the job, then you're well on the way to getting that job.

In the next thirty days, you will be spending hours, days, and weeks talking to hundreds of people, many of them strangers. So you must be organized about what you have to offer an employer—what your strengths are, what's going to excite you and the person hiring you.

Assess yourself. Focus on yourself, learn *exactly* what you have to solve a need or needs for an employer. Make a list of the jobs you've held from age eighteen until now. What did you, in general, like or dislike? What were the specific tasks you performed? Were there special skills needed? Look for a trend, a profile of your career.

Sample Assessment

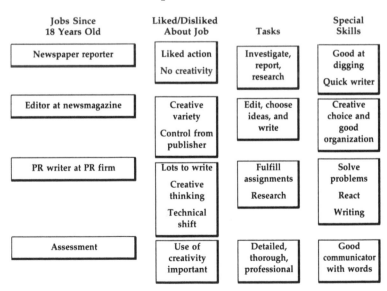

Jobs Since 18 Years Old	Liked/Disliked About Job	Tasks	Special Skills
Newspaper reporter	Liked action No creativity	Investigate, report, research	Good at digging Quick writer
Editor at newsmagazine	Creative variety Control from publisher	Edit, choose ideas, and write	Creative choice and good organization
PR writer at PR firm	Lots to write Creative thinking Technical shift	Fulfill assignments Research	Solve problems React Writing
Assessment	Use of creativity important	Detailed, thorough, professional	Good communicator with words

Using this example, create your own chart. What strengths stand out? What are you good at? What do you like to do?

Now ask your friends and people you've worked with what they think are your strengths. Get some honesty. You may learn that what you think you are and what you project are very different! You may feel you are a "number cruncher," but your friends and co-workers may see you primarily as a really great "people person." So why sell yourself short? Good managers are prized.

You're going to put a tremendous effort into finding a job, so why waste it finding a job other than exactly the one you want? The better the fit, the more you will accomplish, the happier you will be, and the happier your employer will be with your performance. Don't be driven by successive job opportunities that may be offered to you by an employer; be driven by your job goal.

Stay focused. The best weapon for cracking the Hidden Job Market is focus. Retain that focus. You don't want to bounce around and appear to be indecisive. You have a better shot at finding a job if you are prepared.

This next list will help continue the process of defining the job *goal* you want. Your goal is for you to choose, but it helps to have total family support. For which items on the list are there definite answers and on which items can you be flexible?

- geographical location—national versus local hometown versus region
- doing what you do now or total career switch
- salary requirements—higher, lower, same
- change from one industry to another
- change from private industry to government or academia

- profit or nonprofit
- large or small employer
- self-employed or not self-employed
- consulting or staff position

Prioritize the answers from the above list. Is geography more important than salary? Do you want to continue what you are doing now? In any case, you are looking for the key factors that help define your job goal. You want to pick your top *two criteria* for your job search. Picking all nine from the list above does nothing to help you focus—as a matter of fact, it dooms you to failure.

The Right Number of Job Criteria: 2

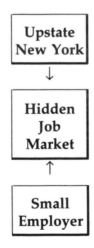

Too Many Job Criteria

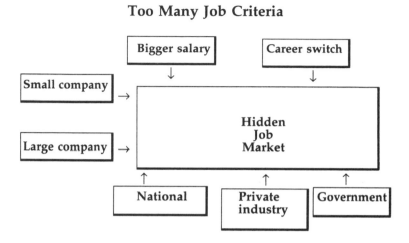

Don't put too many eggs in your basket now. You might feel that looking everywhere increases your chances of getting a job. One of this book's principles is that you need to focus a *quality effort* into fewer companies and the job you want, rather than spreading yourself so thin that you will get a job you become tired of in a short time.

Go back to your list of past experiences. Prioritize what you are good at, what you like to do, and your marketable skills. Compare this list with your friends' opinions of your qualities.

As an example, look at the writer we charted on page 21 in the Sample Assessment.

Writer's Assessment:

Good at: *Detailed and professional; able to research*

Likes to do: *Creative writing*
Skills: *Excellent writer*
Friends say: *Good "talker/presenter"; articulate and takes direction*

Now you write down *your* profile.
Let's see what this writer's ideal job goal is:

1. **Geographic**   Washington, DC
2. **Career**   Speech writer
3. **Salary**   Same salary or less
4. **Industry**   Flexible—elected officials or industry
5. **Size of employer** Flexible
6. **Self-employed**   Flexible

This person has now defined his or her job goals under the top two criteria.

TWO-CRITERIA EXAMPLE

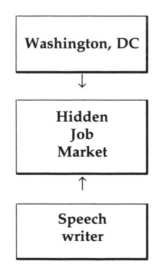

Notice *"self-employed"* is not one of the two criteria. Our writer feels she may be put on staff or put to work on a project basis. Flexibility, however, will create more research work to determine the *needs* of possible employers. Here, having flexibility increases the probability for employment within your Number-One Job Goal.

Look back at the writer's sample assessment on page 20. Certainly, being able to do research and being described as a good creative writer sounds good—and as a bonus, this writer has been told he or she is articulate and a "good talker." Isn't that what speeches are? Good talk?

Look back on your own chart. Assess your strengths. Prioritize your Number-One Job Goal. Be sure it fits your strengths.

What are your top *two criteria*?

CHAPTER 6

The Hidden Job Market

C'mon in! The gate's open!

Introduction

That Helpless Feeling

So you open the morning paper and wow! There's an ad for a job you would be perfect for! You fax off your resume by 9:00 A.M.—only to find the job is already filled.

How did that happen?

You call the personnel department of A&B Company and you are told, "We have no openings." A week later a fellow co-worker who was let go with you gets a job at A&B!

How did that happen?

There's a place you'd really like to work, but you intelligently don't apply because you've read they just laid off 7,500 people. The following month your neighbor gets a great offer to work there.

How did that happen?

You're still out of work.
Why?

Parts of the job market are right in front of your eyes—classified ads, job listings, and personnel departments, for example—but the part you see is just a small total of the jobs that are available, because virtually 80 percent of all jobs are found in the Hidden Job Market. Seventy-five percent of all jobs will not be apparent to you. You will miss them unless you search using the techniques in this book.

Employers don't advertise or even use their personnel department for most jobs because:

- Confidentiality—they don't want the rest of the company to know.
- They already have a pool of people to choose from.
- The job could be a job "waiting to happen," for example:
  - new growth needing new talent
  - need to replace management
  - someone leaves (could fill internally)
  - specific business problems
  - reluctance to bring in an unknown, a risk—someone will hire her college roommate over a hotshot off the street
  - change in philosophy from management

- It's a big-deal process to wade through a ton of résumés.
- They want to retain recruiters.
- Internal politics—one department doesn't want another to know.

Employers are cautious. Hiring the right people, from receptionist to president, can be one of the most important factors contributing to a company's profitable success. They will weigh three major issues before they talk to anyone:

- Risk
- Cost
- Timing

Employers often will "hide" a job until they find a candidate who fits their criteria. Risk is generally the deciding factor. There must be a comfort level before they will commit.

Ideally, the candidate—*you*—is someone they know. The more they know about you, the more their risk is minimized. You need to make yourself a known entity to them or you will not be hired. So you must find out who is doing the hiring and find ways to make this person feel you are the least risky candidate for the job.

The Hidden Job Market is a dynamic, ever-changing, fluid group of people with needs, and parts of it are found inside *any size* organization. The ebb and flow of the process causes job openings and the filling of these jobs all the time, even in the worst recession.

You want to be able to locate these openings as or before they occur and be a candidate *before* the position is filled. To do that, you have to be talking to *a lot* of decision makers in the Hidden Job Market. You want timing to be on *your* side. You're not waiting around!

Now, how do you even begin to tap into the Hidden

Job Market when all these people are unknown to you and openings are unknown to you? That's what you are learning from this book and will accomplish with the Thirty-Day Action Plan. Remember, the fact is there are people who are creating job openings and have the power to hire you. *These people are, in essence, the Gatekeepers to your future.*

You are going to:

1. Find the Gatekeeper.*
2. Judge the timing for an opening.
3. Have the Gatekeeper open the gate to you.

Now, let's step up to the gate!

---

*Here, Gatekeeper is not used to mean a secretary to a higher-placed individual but the higher-placed individual.

CHAPTER 7

He Said That You Said That She Said

If you don't know where you are going,
any path will get you there.

Before you read on, please do a reality check. We're assuming you have defined your Number-One Job Goal, you have a clear, concise idea of what you want to do, and your top two criteria have been selected.

The odds are against you—face it!

If you had only one phone call to find a job, how could you possibly determine who to call? It's impossible to pinpoint that person with just one phone call. It's impossible to find the job that fulfills your Number-One Job Goal by just conventional means. Why?

- Seventy-five percent of the job openings are hidden. The odds are against you!
- The jobs that are open and not hidden, everyone knows about. Want ads in the *New York Times* or the *Wall Street Journal* get anywhere between 500 and 2,000 applicants. The odds are against you!
- Many jobs are filled using a recruiter. I love recruiters. They *live* in the Hidden Job Market, but you don't know them and they don't know you. The odds are against you!
- Many jobs are posted or put in the paper just as a matter of following company policy. They are really already filled.
- Several ads in the papers are placed by recruiters to increase their stable of job candidates (there is no job or it has been filled).
- Timing is critical. Your response was too late in the selection process.
- The people hiring don't know you. *Everyone* submits a good résumé. The risks of picking you are too high.
- The ad in the paper describes you to a T. You apply. The rejection letter says there are people better qualified than you. It turns out the ad did not accurately reflect what they wanted.

The stories go on and on. And nothing *you* do increases the odds in your favor.

The Ideal Situation

The ideal situation is that a department head decides that he or she needs help. You find out that this Gatekeeper is beginning to have some thoughts about creating a position. His or her best friend recommends you. You talk to this Gatekeeper. You are less of a risk because of this friend's recommendation, so the Gatekeeper listens to you. He likes what he hears. You offer more strengths than he thought. You have done what he wants done before. He doesn't even interview anyone else (or if he does, it only confirms you as a better choice). You have sold him on *you!* You have helped define the job, working conditions, and salary. You have your Number-One Job Goal!

You made the odds work in your favor. That is what our strategy is all about. Meeting and talking with enough people so that you:

- Find the Gatekeepers.
- Find them as the job is forming or early on in the process.
- Know enough about your industry, the company, the people hiring, the problems that need to be addressed, the solutions.
- Reduce the risk of being an unknown by being referred by people the Gatekeeper trusts.

There is a misconception out there that *companies* have jobs for people. Not true! *People* have jobs for people. You aren't really dealing with a company or place of work. You are going to get your job from *people*. It is not sufficient to contact the company's human resources department (but *you* know that).

Once you realize it is people who provide you with a job, not a building or annual report, you can get control of the process and have it work for you. You contact people and have them tell you who the Gatekeepers are.

Sounds like good old networking. It is networking.

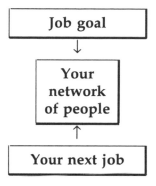

Because it is people who hand out jobs, this book is aimed at getting you in contact with people. Clearly, the more people you contact, the higher your chances of success in finding the job you want in thirty days. The fact is, you can have up to a thousand new friends helping you find a job! We'll get more specific about networking in "Positioning You," where you'll learn whom to contact and how to contact—we've even supplied scripts for you to use.

The Hidden Job Market *stays* hidden unless you have a very organized and methodical approach to help increase your odds.

CHAPTER 8

It Becomes Not Just *Who* You Know but *What* You Know

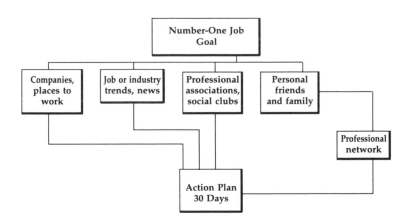

Number-One Job Goal: You know that, right?

There are three basic weapons to use to attack the Hidden Job Market: knowledge, networking, and targeted effort. It is not easy process; it's time-consuming and has its ups and downs. But it works. You'll make it work!

Places to Work

You probably have selected either a geographic goal, an industry goal, or a job function as one of your top criteria. This helps you limit your search. You must be realistic (an underwater basket weaver in the desert probably is a little limiting, for example), and your research and networking will soon tell you whether you are. If you feel that you may have that situation before you start, you may want to alter your goal slightly (perhaps underwater basket weaver in *fresh water*, in which case lakes and streams are the places to look).

At first, you will want to identify every possible company that could be a candidate. No matter how exhaustive your search or how many resources you use, you will not have the total list of companies that offer you job possibilities. The reasons why are simple:

- New companies are being formed every day.
- You will unconsciously and consciously rule out companies for logical and illogical reasons because you don't have the time to know everything about every company.
- Your conception of a particular company may be incorrect, so you will not add it to your list.
- Industry information—directories, databases, and associations—by its very nature is merely a snapshot of the industry.

But don't worry. You don't have to know everyone or have perfect knowledge. You need only enough contacts and enough knowledge to present you with a job that fits your Number-One Job Goal.

Research

Let's focus on the process of identifying companies and see how people and resources can be used to construct your lists of companies.

The key sources of identifying companies will be books, magazines, and other periodicals. Your library will become very familiar to you during this process. Befriend your librarian, and she'll never forget you! If you have friends at large companies who have libraries, get them to help you locate materials. Business libraries are geared to service these requests. You will probably not be allowed access to these company libraries, but some of your friends who work there will have access. Also, universities have libraries that you can often use. You may not be able to check books out, but often the books are reference books that can't be removed from the library anyway.

Some of the library sources you will use are as follows (these go from the general to the specific):

General

The National Directory of Addresses and Telephone Numbers, Concord Reference Books.

The Directory of Directories, Gale Research Company.

Guide to American Directories, B. Klein Publications.

Moody's Industrial Review.

Consultants and Consulting Organizations Directory, Gale Research Company.

Business

Directory of Corporate Affiliations, National Register Publishing Co.

Standard & Poor's Register of Corporations, Standard & Poor's Register of Corporations.

Dun & Bradstreet Million Dollar Directory, Dun's Marketing Services.

Fortune 500 Companies, Fortune magazine.

Inc. magazine and many others have lists of new, small, and fast-growing companies.

Regional, State, Local

Regional or state industrial directories.

Visit your local Chamber of Commerce. Look at business sections of the local papers.

Associations

Encyclopedia of Associations, Gale Research Company.

Periodicals and Publications

Forbes, Fortune, Inc., Business Week, Barron's, Newsweek, Time.

Industry-Specific Publications

Standard Rate and Data Service. (SRDS) Advertising agencies and PR firms use this publication. It will give you *all* the trade magazines and periodicals by industry classification.

You will find more information on these resources and others when you get to the Thirty-Day Action Plan.

Networking

As you begin to network, many of the company leads you develop will be from your contacts. Get together with other people who are out of work or recently back to work. They will share company names, even contacts, with you. If someone was just successful in getting a position, his or her list of companies and contacts might be available to you.

Think of companies who supply your industry. They will know about companies in your area and elsewhere. They have knowledge of new companies, small companies, trends in the industry, who's growing, and key management personnel. They are an excellent source of information. Consultants are also a good source of information and contacts.

Industry Trends

It is important to know what is going on in your field. Don't forget you will be talking with Gatekeepers. They will think of things on a grand scale, and you want to be able to converse at their level. These people like to talk about issues, unresolved questions that everyone is looking for the answer to, such as:

- Competitive strategies (how to get a leg up on the competition)
- Environment
- How to reduce costs

You get the idea. All of the industry magazines will be full of the issues and the answers. As a matter of fact, you want to cut out key articles to use with your résumé and cover letter to these Gatekeepers. It will help differentiate you from the others. It will be something to talk about in face-to-face meetings.

All the information you gather will help you ask smarter questions, make you more confident, make you more interesting to listen to, and best of all, provide you with leads, contacts, and a sense of belonging.

Professional Associations and Clubs

There is at least one association for every profession or industry. The associations exist for networking. Consultants use them to meet contacts to get work. Company individuals use them to learn, find jobs, discuss mutual problems, develop leadership skills, and gain a sense of identity. You will find that many of the association leaders like to talk. Almost all of them will be willing to help (if you don't put them on the spot for a job!).

Go to meetings, get on committees, get involved. People will see what you can do. Almost all Gatekeepers are members of associations. Many of the up-and-coming professionals are members. Don't be afraid to get involved.

Social clubs—from bridge to country clubs—are a great way to network. Everyone has hobbies and interests; exercise at social clubs, play golf, play tennis, talk to the person next to you on the Stairmaster, play racquetball, bowl in a league. Use these opportunities to work off frustrations and to meet people. At social clubs you get to know people on a different ground level. The socializing will also help you deal with the feelings of isolation you have because you are not working.

Personal Friends and Family

These people are your greatest asset. They usually can't give you a job, but they will provide support and they know other people.

First, they will provide a nonthreatening way for you to start networking. They will review your résumé and your networking scripts and give you feedback. They represent your sanity check. Some of the people will actually be part of your professional network because they became your friends through work. If a few are also unemployed, they will become your closest support group. Share feelings, contacts, frustrations. Strangely enough, this experience will bring you closer to your family and friends. Be sure you guide your friends and family on *exactly* how you want them to support you, and you should be sensitive to their needs as well.

Don't forget that your friends want to help. Use them and let them know what they mean to you.

Professional Network

Everyone has one. It's the group of business acquaintances just outside your close work friends: your boss, his or her boss, co-workers who know you're good, contacts you have made with workers outside your company. These are people you can call on, people who will also give you their honest opinions. They know Gatekeepers; they know you. Have them introduce you—what could be better? They will tell the Gatekeeper you are good, and they will tell you all about the Gatekeeper.

This group is your strongest link to the world

outside your former place of employment. Use it well. Don't squander it. If you were lucky enough to be in sales, customer service, purchasing, etc. where you had a lot of contact with people outside your company, you are one step ahead of everyone else. If you know these people in your former company, use them. They can give you lists of contacts.

POSITIONING YOU

Get Ready for the Thirty-Day Action Plan

Set up an organized approach to develop your own network with lists and follow-up for entry into The Hidden Job Market

Set Up Your Home Office

Create Your Network—Get Referent Power

Do Your Test Marketing

CHAPTER 9

Welcome to Your New Office

It begins with a phone. The telephone is the single most important tool necessary to enter the Hidden Job Market quickly. To save money, order *The National Directory of Addresses and Telephone Numbers*, (206) 828–4777. They take credit cards and the price is about $35.

Where you put the phone is important. It should be in a place where you won't be distracted by a TV and where you can have privacy. If you share the phone with other people, the phone line should be yours from eight to five. Be firm about that. For those of you who are looking nationally, don't forget that time zones add to the hours you can call if you plan your calls by time zone. This means that the hours before nine can be used to call east and the hours after five can be used to call west, and even lunchtime can be productive calling time. The phone should be on a table that can hold your file system, pads, and a directory or two. You should be sitting in a chair that is comfortable all day. Lots of light. Cheery, happy. Make a corner or room for yourself that suits you. Some people like to hang a mirror so they can look at themselves. An inspirational poster. A window. A clock.

Go through the following list. Whatever has a ★, put on your Must Have list. In developing this list for the Thirty-Day Action Plan, we have done everything possible to make your job search as economical as possible. If you have an office and phone given to you for a while from your former employer, you're lucky! All of us need:

Office: Can you do the Thirty-Day Action Plan from the kitchen table? Sure. Have boxes to put things into at the end of the day. Shoo everyone away from the kitchen except for designated times.

Telephone: Any phone will do. Touchtone is best because so many companies have electronic voice messaging, which requires interaction by using the touchtone system. If you're lucky, many of the people you call will be at 800 numbers. To repeat, make sure you have control of the phone from eight to five and whenever else you need it.

Telephone answering machine: When you are getting close to an interview or confirming a meeting, you may be spending time out of your office, so consider the value. Make sure your message is professional: don't get cute. This is also not the time to blast the "1812 Over-ture." Your name and number are fine!

Résumé: Make it as professional as possible. It is an invaluable investment. It has to look good. There are many places that will design and print it for you. Consider customizing it when you learn about a specific job. *No* amount of special effort is overdoing it if there is a job prospect close at hand. Writing an effective résumé is a science. Research what experts say, look at different formats. In any case, your résumé should be concise, very easy to read, and geared to your job objective. No fluff. Read the test-market chapter of this book (Chapter 11) before you have hundreds of copies made. Think of the employer and *his or her* point of view. Are you an action person who solved problems? What can you do that the employer needs to have done? And keep it short. Remember our exercise: what are the key skills you have delivered over several jobs? You decide what is most important. Your list of skills is probably too long to fit on your résumé, but do not lose the longer list. Some of these skills may be just what the Gatekeeper is looking for in a candidate. This list will be good for your interviewing process, as well as for customizing your résumé.

Stationery: You need paper and envelopes. See if you can get the same paper you used for your résumé. If you are looking for a top management position, you really should have stationery and envelopes printed with your name, address, phone number, and fax number in the same typeface as your résumé. Go first-class. At any level of job, you want to show an image of professionalism. Call several quickie printing places for prices. It shows your attention to detail to have printed envelopes and letterhead. Besides, you can always use the stationery after you have a job.

    If it simply isn't in your budget, then just be sure to deliver neat businesslike letters. As a gentle reminder—probably not necessary—here's the format you should use for a business letter:

JANE BROWN

---

123 Any Street   Phone: (123) 456–7890
Any Town, Anywhere 12345   Fax: (123) 456–7891
↓
3
Date
↓
3
Name
Title
Company
Address 1
Address 2
City/State/Zip Code
↓
2
Salutation:

Body of letter

↓
2
Complimentary close,
↓
4

Your name
Enclosure notation

Typewriter: Your correspondence should be typed. If you don't know how to type, find someone who can. Envelopes should be typed, too. Never, ever send out a letter with any typos in it. You are going to be writing cover letters for your résumé, thank-you notes, confirmation of meetings, and so on. Once in a while, you can hand-write to people you feel would appreciate a more personal note.

Word processor: Can make your correspondence much easier. You can also compose form letters to use over and over. Try leasing or borrowing a word processor from a friend for thirty days. It also allows you to use a very professional typeface. I like 12-point Times Roman—always a safe bet. Don't go wild on the choices. Pick one typeface and stick with it. A printer is also a must, but only if you decide to use the best. Stay away from anything but letter-quality printing.

If you are a computer jock, there are also programs available for sales people with call plans and contact profiles (addresses, phone numbers, notes, hobbies). They can be used if you want to do this all electronically. **Warning:** Computer networking is no substitute for personal contacting. Remember, *people* give people jobs.

Fax: A nice luxury for instantly getting a résumé or note in hand. We suggest you get a machine that is a phone, answering machine, and fax all in one. Call around for prices. There are some good deals out there!

3 x 5 cards: Your network needs to be stored. On each card put the contact's name, title, company, address, phone number, and fax number, the first date called, who referred you, and any other information you have about this person, including personal information (e.g., "Yale medical school, jogs, 16 handicap"). Also note follow-up date, checking to be sure that your contact will be in on that date.

Flexible folder: You can buy one at any office supply store. It is a large accordion-style pocket file with dividers labeled 1 through 31 on the pockets. You will be keeping track of your networking journey through the Hidden Job Market *day by day.* This is your tickle file. A tickle file is a kind of follow-up file—organized by date. It must stay *organized.* File cards and notes go in it, under the follow-up date (Day 1–31). Those calls where you were not successful in reaching your party are filed in the next day's pocket or the date your contact will be back.

Manilla folders **(two sets):** Buy enough for A–Z. You will keep research on companies, people, and industry trends alphabetically. The second set is to keep correspondence in, alphabetically, by company.

Shoe box: Don't laugh! It's the easiest and neatest way to file your 3 x 5 cards that aren't in your tickle file.

Pads of paper: Notes will be taken, letters will be drafted.

Calendar: A big and easy-to-read desk calendar that has week-at-a-glance pages. This book will help you keep track of meetings and so on.

Library: Have the librarian show you how to access information. You can make copies there, too.

Daily paper: Be informed about the world around you. Don't spend a lot of time on the classifieds, though!

Plenty of pens, tape, staples, and paper clips.

Working alone takes initiative. You have to fuel yourself to keep going. You'll find a certain exhilaration talking to the outside world that will give you energy and, yes, hope.

Don't become lonely and isolated. While you *are* dedicated to the daily tasks, be sure you get out to see people. Have lunch with friends—both in and out of work! Take a walk. Get out of your office. There are lots of useful excuses! If you have a person from General Motors Company on your network list, go visit a GM dealership and see the new cars, talk to the salespeople, and see what you can learn.

Gather support from your friends and family. Lean on them, talk to them about your progress; they *want* you to share what you're up to, how you're doing. Remind them if you have to that you are, in fact, *back to work,* because looking for work is a full-time endeavor.

How to Use Your Office: A Sample Work Day

A typical day will begin with a review of your calendar. Do you have research at the library? A lunch meeting? An informational meeting?

Look to your base list of contacts and tickle file. Be sure you have twenty calls to make, plus those people you didn't reach yesterday. Gather your 3 x 5 cards.

A typical call can be as simple as the following:

"Good morning. This is Rick Williams. Is Mr. Gate in, please?"

"No, he's not."

"When may I get back to him, please?"

"Next Monday afternoon."

"I'll call back then. Thank you."

If you have a strong link—for example, references such as a person's name, perhaps a member of an association—you may want to leave your name. Secretaries can really be a big help to you. It's *fine* to bare your soul a little. Tell the secretary why you are calling. *You are not calling for a job,* but you are out of work and you have been referred to Mr. Gate for advice. Perhaps he knows other possible contacts. Use a human side to your approach, and you'll get some deserved sympathy.

Record on the 3 x 5 card the date to follow up. Put it in the appropriate tickle day in your expandable file. Note any other information that you learn—for example, if he was out of town in Arizona. Jot it down.

When you do get a response—such as *"Sure, send me your résumé; I'll come up with a few people you can call"*— then you must follow up right away. Move the 3 x 5 card six business days ahead, three days for a fax. Type your cover letter and send (or fax) it with your résumé.

A similar letter (as illustrated in Letter A on the following page) with a general business article should conclude by mentioning the article that is enclosed and, in fact, that you would like to talk about it when you call. The last sentence of *any* letter should be about what is going to happen next.

My Name

My Address
My City/State/Zip Code   My Phone Number

Date

Mr. Gatekeeper
Title
Company
Address 1
Address 2
City/State/Zip Code

Dear Mr. Gatekeeper:

Thank you for talking with me today.

I appreciate your taking time to consider my situation. Your comments about the hotel business in Southern California were very helpful to me.

I enclose my résumé, which highlights my areas of expertise. I hope that it may help you pinpoint whom you feel I should call.

I will long remember your consideration and advice and will follow up in a week.

Best regards,

Me

enclosure

You do not want to drop the ball with Referent Power. Quick follow-up will help people remember you and will reinforce their perception of you as a professional truly in need of their help. You are not wasting their time!

Continue this process through twenty or more calls. Be *very* detailed and organized with your tickle file.

Thank-you notes for face-to-face meetings should go out the day of the meeting or the next day at the very latest.

And now for your research. You will be reading articles and making notes, such as a summary of the five major business points. You may form an opinion, which could give you something to talk about. This material, however, does not replace your policy of getting referred and building contacts. Keep research files together in a drawer or box with dividers.

CHAPTER 10

Referent Power: Creating Your Network

*Use it wisely
and you'll get that job.*

Referent Power is a brand-new term we came up with for an age-old practice, and that is:

People graciously lending you their power (their reference and their contacts) so you have more power to get ahead.

You are going to find hundreds of new friends who will use their power to help you find a job. *Why will all these people help me? Whom do I approach? What do I want them to do for me? How do I approach those people?* These may be some of the questions that occur to you.

Let's back up. You'll recall that it's people who hire people, not companies. You will network using Referent Power to get through to the Hidden Job Market. You know that people are looking to reduce perceived risk in hiring—they want to hire someone they know. People will ask their professional counterparts if they know of someone right for the job. You also know how hard it is to find the job you want. So you know you have to talk to *many* people, many Gatekeepers.

<h2 style="text-align:center">The Egg Chart: Referent Power
and The Hidden Job Market</h2>

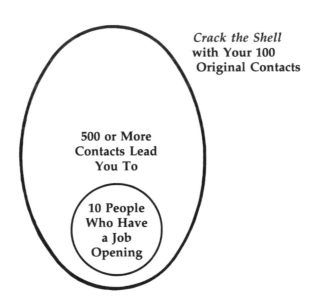

Crack the Shell
**with Your 100
Original Contacts**

**500 or More
Contacts Lead
You To**

**10 People
Who Have
a Job
Opening**

The Hidden Job Market looks like an egg. There's a shell of protection, holding the egg white inside, which surrounds the hidden yolk. Only by going successfully through the layers of egg white will you reach the yolk; only a few Gatekeepers hold the key to your Number-One Job Goal.

Why will all these people help me?

To begin with, generally you have been referred by someone they know. There is a friendly, professional (although often distant) link. Also people are often flattered if you turn to them for advice. No matter whether you're a line foreman or a CEO for a *Fortune* 500 company, you should be able to ask for advice from anyone. Plus, most people know that with a flick of a company finger, *they* could be out of work. At least to be on the safe side of good business manners, they should listen to you. How *long* they will listen will be up to you, and will be based on your research and the presentation of your goals. We'll talk more about that in the Thirty-Day Action Plan.

You aren't asking them for money, for personal details, or even for a job. You aren't threatening them. All you are asking for is a little of their time and power; the power they have to give you is inside information, more contacts, potential opportunities, and the use of their name. They have nothing to lose, and in fact, smart people will add *you* to their own list of potentially influential people. People will respond if you are enthusiastic, upbeat, excited. Drive, clear direction, and stated goals are impressive and demand attention. You will be surprised at the length of some conversations.

Whom do I approach?

Your first list will be as large as possible— acquaintances. Pull out your personal phone book.

List A: Friends, relatives, and personal professionals. Your lawyer, your accountant, your Sunday school teacher, the kid who cuts the grass (whose dad could be president of your Dream Company). People you see often: the owner of your favorite restaurant, your hairdresser, your babysitter, your neighbors. Lots and lots of everyday friends who *may* be able to help you to penetrate and enter the Hidden Job Market.

List B: Professionals in your line of work. Old bosses who liked you, people who worked for you. Suppliers, competitors, customers, clients, people you know in related fields. Say you create advertising for billboards; put down the person you know who sells the space on the billboard.

Write **List A** and **List B** on your pad of paper. Decide which of these people are social, professional, and informational contacts.

EXAMPLES:

Social	Parents, neighbors, paper boy, hairdresser, and so on.
Professional	Vice president of sales for a competitor to your old company or place of work.
Informational	Owner of a company that trucks the product to market for a company in your targeted industry.

Now you have three lists to begin your networking.

These three lists together should total no less than one hundred contacts.

Referent Power works best with this axiom: *Contact at the highest level.* In fact, try to get to people who will be higher than those in your Number-One Job Goal. It is my recommendation that you go two or three levels above the level where you will be reporting. People listen to their boss and their boss's boss. They will want to please their boss by listening to you, since you were referred by the higher boss. You may need several contacts to identify people at this high level.

You can scale down your list after a round or two of calls, as you begin to see which contact is getting you closest to your Number-One Job Goal.

What do I want them to do for me?

First, you want them to listen. Then you want them to give you what you want, which could be:

- information about what's going on in the industry
- information about the company
- knowledge about special skills or education required in their industry
- ideas on how your strengths would be appropriate for their type of business
- advice that includes at least two more contacts they know
- reviewing your résumé to know you better
- a meeting

Chances are (like 99 percent!) that whoever you talk to does not have an empty office to fill at that minute. So all you want is some real helpful advice, some idea of where the gates are in the Hidden Job Market. Ideally, you want your contacts to refer you to *their* contacts. *Always* verify that you can use their name. You'll see, day by day in the Thirty-Day Action Plan, how to get your network to help you.

Face-to-face meetings, necessarily short and informational, are great. Many times a face-to-face meeting can solidify Referent Power. Your contact may like you more and may take a larger interest in your future (which may include a job at his or his best friend's company).

How to I approach my network?

With a positive attitude. Charming. Professional. Humble. Organized about goals and identified skills. Nice. Ready to listen. Not pushy, but really focused. Respectful. Upbeat. Perfect. Whew! Isn't looking for a job hard work?

Fact is, the network person you have been referred to, especially at a high level, probably gets millions of calls from people out of work. This person, this Gate-keeper, will be considering who referred you. The tone of your voice will instantly set up a willingness to help or be a turn-off. You can start with honesty. However, your honesty should immediately include the fact that you aren't calling him or her for a job (that would be dumb). Whoever you are calling should know *why* you are calling (you are asking them to help you by looking at your résumé and giving you some names when you call back).

Find a way, *any* way, to not be all "yackety-yackety" about yourself. For example, a lawyer calling a law firm might mention a similar case, if his research revealed his contact was working on a specific case. They would compare notes, and our job hunter would be rewarded with three new contacts to call in the other firm.

Just be straight. Here's a typical sample script (no pressure please—and you are sincere):

YOU: *(Dial number) Ring ring.*
BOB: Bob Jones.
YOU: Mr. Jones, this is Jeff Stuart calling. Mark Field suggested I call you. He said you know more about the hotel business than anyone!
BOB: Call me Bob.
YOU: I'd really appreciate some advice for my

career. I've spent the last six years managing hotels, I believe similar to yours, that actively host conventions. I'm looking to put my hotel convention management expertise to work out West. How's the convention business out there? Who's growing?

BOB: *(He tells you.)*

YOU: That's good to know! In any case, I just don't know anyone out there. I'd like to send you my résumé and I'd greatly appreciate it if you could suggest anyone who you think might be interested in me.

BOB: Sure.

YOU: I'd like to call you in a week or so to follow up. Is Tuesday okay?

BOB: Sure. Glad to help.

YOU: Thanks! Talk to you soon.

CHAPTER 11

The Test Market

The purpose of this chapter is to make you comfortable with networking and to test your scripts with your close friends and family, to get you familiar with the routine and how your office will work, to get the butterflies out of your stomach, to gain confidence, to gain valuable feedback, to shape your story with the help of friends, and to personalize the process to fit you.

First, the Number-One Job Goal.

Review this with family first. Have them understand what you are doing. If you are going on a *national* search, you must have their support—spouse, children, and parents. Do they think you'll be good in that job? Is it you? (A word of caution: They think you can do anything!)

Next, talk to friends, former bosses, and if you're lucky, a few people who actually are doing the job you targeted. Do they feel you're right for the job? Did you learn from the people that are doing your job what the frustrations are? What the boring part of the job is? What's exciting? What skills are needed? See if you can talk to the boss and ask him what *he* looks for when hiring for that position.

Listen for Bells to Go Off!!

Good Bell (from people or inside you)	**Questionable Bell** (from people or inside you)
That fits you to a tee.	Sales is for me, but I hate traveling.
You're the best at that.	Are you sure you're ready for that?
You always seemed happiest when you were doing that.	No kidding! I never thought you wanted to do that!
I can't wait to start!	My best friend has the job and he thinks I would hate it.
I've done that before and have done it well.	I think you can do better than that.
Yes, there are parts of the job I don't like, but they're minor.	
That job is close to what I think you should do, but have you ever thought of . . .	

You get the idea. Listen for the bells to tell you if your Number-One Job Goal is on track.

Second, the résumé.

Remember your last job review. What were your strong points? Your weak ones? Don't list weak skills as strong—you will only disappoint your new employer and you will *not* come off as confident as you will if you show that you know your weaknesses.

Get your friends to review your résumé for typos. One undetected typo, one messy blotch, or one nonprofessional statement can be disastrous. Remember, résumés are used to screen you *out*, not in. I was asked about a résumé that shows three jobs in three years. The truth about this person was that he was brought in to do turnarounds at these three companies. Everyone knows that once you do a turnaround, you are usually let go so the company can mend under new leadership. My suggestion was to state that he was a consultant for three years and to list these companies as clients. Your references will back you. I am *not* suggesting that you be dishonest, just that you cast the most favorable light on the facts in your résumé. In this case, this person was excellent at what he did in the turnarounds. It was the *appearance* of his résumé that screened him out; not his actual job performance.

Be absolutely confident in your résumé and be able to answer any questions about it. Know it better than anyone.

Third, the process of networking.

Pick ten of your contacts from the list. Use them to test your performance in networking and in your operation of the office. These should be people who will readily talk to you—friends, acquaintances. This "Test of Ten" should be deliberately easy and comfortable.

First, make sure your 3 x 5 cards are filled in:

- name
- address
- phone number
- date of contact
- follow-up date
- information on company (if you have it)
- personal information

(The last two categories are primarily for people you don't know.)

Make the calls, use the script. Most of your friends will give you contacts over the phone rather than wait until you send a résumé, but do include a couple of people who will receive your résumé. For those people, do a cover letter and send a résumé. On the 3 x 5 card make note of the date contacted, the follow-up date, and any other pertinent information.

For those who gave you contacts, have other 3 x 5 cards ready to record the information on the new contacts. *Do not forget to list who referred you to the contact.* It is hard to pick up the phone for the first few calls. Did people call you back? How many calls did you have to make to get five people? Did you get all ten?

Finally, the Thirty-Day Action Plan.

You should be ready. Now for your final checklist:

- Are you confident?
- Do you understand how to use your office?
- Do you feel comfortable with the process?
- Do you know the scripts?

Be ready to take each day at a time. If you focus on the overall task, it will cause gridlock. Some days it will feel as though you didn't get very far, but you are already far ahead of others; far ahead of the millions of people who don't have a clue as to how to enter the Hidden Job Market.

PITCHING YOU

The Thirty-Day Action Plan to Get the Job You Want

Building a Network of Hundreds of Contacts into the Hidden Job Market

Real-Life Success Stories

The Thirty-Day
Action Plan

We suggest you start this Monday.

Before you pick up the phone, be sure you have completed the preparation in Positioning You.

Be prepared for the duration of the battle for entry into the Hidden Job Market. It's thirty long business days.

Your test-market experience should have given you practice in approaching people for help.

Don't worry if you sound a little rusty, a little—or even a lot—out of tune. Your presentation will become smooth and friendly. The key is to be friendly and honest. Just be yourself.

You will soon have a hundred 3 x 5 cards filled out with contacts in your shoe box, arranged in order of your estimation of their helpfulness in finding your Number-One Job Goal.

Please, please, please, don't give up. A wonderful job is out there or will be out there for you if only you can find it and position yourself as a great choice for the employer.

Take it one day at a time, stay upbeat, and soon hardworking you will be very lucky!

WEEK ONE

Crack the Hidden Job Market

Target Places of Work

Do Intense Research on Industry and Occupation

DAY 1

Good morning!

Today's Quote

> *The dawn speeds a man on his journey,*
> *and speeds him too in his work.*
> —Hesiod

Today's Focus

You have already done your test market, which should have given you some experience. This will help you in today's task.

We will stay in the realm of contacts you know and will not be contacting strangers today. Besides the specific goals you see below, the object of today is to help you begin feeling comfortable telling people you are out of work and enlisting their help.

Today's Helpful Hint

Keep your mind open to evaluate ideas your contacts will talk about, regardless of how ridiculous they sound!

Today's Goals

- Have twenty of your base-list contacts agree to review your résumé and have each provide you with two new contacts.

- Get as current as possible in your job field.
- Reward yourself with either physical activity, mental relaxation, or psychological support.

Today's Tasks

- Make enough calls to meet the first goal. Prepare and send twenty résumés with personalized cover letters.
- Establish follow-up dates for each contact. If you faxed anyone, plan to recontact in three days. If you contacted by mail, allow six working days before following up.
- Place contacts in appropriate tickle-file date.
- Read today's newspaper. The whole paper.
- Give yourself a gift. Why not start with some exercise? Even a brisk walk around the block will energize you. Do it anytime during the day.

Today's Tickle

None.

Today's Review

Have you prepared your phone scripts? Was it hard to reach people? Have you completed letters with résumés? How did your office setup work? Does it need any changes? What did you learn today that will help you tomorrow?

Today's Emotional Check

- Were you scared?
- Was it frustrating not being able to reach people?
- Did you have to push yourself to make each call?
- Was the last call easier than the first?

Today's True Story

The Dog Ate My Résumé

Sandy managed to find the perfect opening at a major computer company for his circuitry repair skills. He was very disappointed to learn from the personnel department that he wasn't a candidate because he didn't have the skills they needed. Sandy was *sure* they had drawn some very wrong conclusions, so he quickly began to network his way in, seeing no fewer than eight people. Eventually, it became apparent that they had lost the second page of his résumé! By this time he had made such an impression he had not one but two opportunities offered to him!

Tomorrow

Plan a trip to the library and read current job-related journals and other publications. Look for industry events and trends that might play to your strengths. Make copies for your FYI file. Continue to research your source materials (for new companies) to look for work.

DAY 2

Good morning!

Today's Quote

> *There's a whining at the threshold—*
> *There's a scratching at the floor—*
> *To work! To work! In Heaven's name!*
> *The wolf is at the door!*
> —Charlotte Perkins Gilman

Today's Focus

We continue, as we do every day, to make our *minimum* twenty contacts. In addition, today we will begin your job-hunting research. The library is where you can start today. Listed are a few resources.

Our first area of investigation will be for general information.

The Directory of Directories—lists all of the directories out there.

Guide to American Directories—similar resource.

Moody's Industry Review—lists top companies by industry/category.

Consultants & Consulting Organizations Directory

Today's Helpful Hint

Use your job goal to focus your research. Don't get off the track!

Today's Goals

- Get twenty more contacts working for you.
- Identify at least five additional directories that will aid you in further research.

Today's Tasks

- Call anyone you were unable to reach yesterday.
- Add to those enough new calls so that you meet the minimum of twenty.
- Establish follow-up dates for each contact.
- Place contacts in appropriate tickle-file pocket by date.
- Go to the library and use directories recommended or similar reference material.

Today's Tickle

None.

Today's Review

After you made your twenty contacts and your follow-up, did you spend the rest of the day at the library? Did you know how to use the directories? Have you used them to identify your next research step?

Today's Emotional Check

- Are you excited? Did you know it would be this much work to find work?
- Have you found your contacts helpful so far?

Today's True Story

Networking?
Any Nine-Year-Old Can Do It

Betsy's husband was out of work. Time for Betsy to sharpen the old clerical skills and get a job. Betsy was *terrible* at networking. She had never done it, had no idea *how* to do it, and on top of that, was not even getting interviews for any of the jobs she read about in the newspapers. One night at dinner, Dave, her nine-year-old son (who attends an *expensive* private school), announced, "Mom! I found you a job!" The kid was networking! Much to her surprise, the next morning she received a call from the school. They were delighted to have her work in their office!

Tomorrow

Back to the library.

DAY 3

Good morning!

Today's Quote

> *All work, even cotton-spinning, is noble; work is alone noble. . . . A life of ease is not for any man, nor for any god.*
> —Thomas Carlyle

Today's Focus

In addition to making your twenty minimum contacts, we will use additional resources at the library to focus on specific companies within our target market.

Directory of Corporate Affiliations—basically an index of the companies that own other companies.

Standard and Poor's Register of Corporations

Directors and Executives—a guide to public companies.

Dun & Bradstreet Million Dollar Directory—a guide to 160,000 small to large public companies.

Fortune 500—companies in *Fortune* magazine.

Today's Helpful Hint

While you should not ignore large companies, most job openings are in companies with between one and five hundred employees.

Today's Goals

- Use the additional directories that you identified yesterday and the ones suggested for today to choose target companies and contacts.
- Twenty more contacts should be working for you.

Today's Tasks

- Call anyone you missed yesterday and add to those enough new calls to reach your twenty minimum.
- Establish follow-up dates for each contact. Send letters and résumés.
- Place contacts in appropriate tickle file.
- Go to the library and use the references you have found, with a focus on finding names to contact at specific companies.

Today's Tickle

Those of you who are faxing will see it is time to call contacts back and get at least two names you can use to network further.

Today's Review

- Are you beginning to see how your research on companies is going to be able to help you target your search?
- Were you able to construct several lists of target companies? Were you able to obtain *at least* several published names of contacts in companies that interest you?
- Did you make your twenty contacts?

Today's Emotional Check

Are you gaining confidence in yourself?

Today's True Story

How Fast Can You Learn Lithuanian?

"Real fast!" That's what an out-of-work U.S. ambassador said when his networking paid off. The honorable person in this story had been globally networking to land one of the greatly coveted ambassadorships. Our man could see a trend in a new market (the "old" Soviet Union), and he prepared himself while focusing his networking. Sure enough, one afternoon there was a need for fifteen new ambassadors. To make a long story short, our man was first in line.

Tomorrow

Research focus will be regional, state, and local. You will be visiting the Chamber of Commerce.

DAY 4

Good morning!

Today's Quote

> *In order that people may be happy in their work, these three things are needed: They must be fit for it. They must not do too much of it. And they must have a sense of success in it.*
> —John Ruskin

Today's Focus

Our job-hunting research will focus on regional, state, and local sources.

In your library, there should be a regional or state industrial directory—for example, *The New England Industrial Directory.* Ask your librarian for regional and local resources.

Visit your local Chamber of Commerce and ask their advice on available additional material. They also may be very helpful at identifying contacts, especially if you are a member. In any case, they may be able to give you a contact at a specific company if you ask.

Today's Helpful Hint

Keep a sharp eye on your local business newspaper's pages, taking note of personnel changes, which will give you names of new people with their new titles and good clues to jobs that have just been vacated.

Today's Goals

- Create list of local companies and contacts.
- Begin to call contacts you do not know from your tickle file (from faxing) and research.

Today's Tasks

- Make your minimum twenty calls. Today may be different because you will be introducing yourself to people you don't know and may not have a reference for. *It is absolutely essential* that you do not ask them for a job. (See script on page 60.)
- Follow up with people you didn't reach yesterday.
- Establish dates for following-up today's contacts.
- Send letters and résumés.
- Go to library for local research.
- Go to Chamber of Commerce. Ask if there are any local associations to contact, such as Sales Executive Association, Women in Communications, and so forth.
- Look in yellow pages for businesses related to your job goal. For example, look under "Market Research" to find firms that do that.

Today's Tickle

If you're faxing, you're tickling.

Today's Review

- Do you have an overview of what's out there locally? Did you contact people you don't know?
- Was the Chamber of Commerce helpful?
- Are you beginning to understand networking and how it operates?

Today's Emotional Check

- Are you overwhelmed?
- Are you getting support from your family?
- Do you feel you'll have the tenacity to do this for thirty days?
- Give yourself a pat on the back for doing well so far.

Today's True Story

John was selling office equipment and had read in the local paper that someone had just been promoted to regional sales manager. He called the promoted person to see if his just-vacated district manager job was still open. Had anyone filled it? John learned that the company was looking to bring in someone from outside to fill the position.

John had the inside information and the job description, and he found out who was the person to call for an interview. He also got a rundown on the job and learned about the boss who could hire him. John got the job.

Tomorrow

We tackle association research. Back to the library!

DAY 5

Good morning!

Today's Quote

> *Work brings its own relief;*
> *He who most idle is*
> *Has most of grief.*
> —Eugene Fitch Ware

Today's Focus

We will complete our first week of research by identifying clubs and associations that will help identify further contacts and help us learn more about your business.

Look for this book in your library:

Encyclopedia of Associations: National Organizations of the U.S. It lists over 19,500 U.S. nonprofit associations and organizations of all kinds—business and trade, political, professional, social, fraternal, educational, ethnic, etc.

Some associations will send you their membership list free (or for a small charge) without your having to join. Call them and see what you can learn. See if you can find someone you know who is a member. Some of you should join because associations are really networks. They exist to be networks. They are like fraternities; once you are in, whatever resources they have are at your fingertips. The most valuable benefit is that when you call someone in the association, you have an established bond. Some of the best job hunters claim this as their secret, so use your clubs and associations.

Today's Helpful Hint

Continue to use your associations *after* you find a job. Make networking continue to work for you the rest of your life.

Today's Goals

- Identify associations pertinent to your job.
- Join an association and/or club.
- Continue to call contacts you don't know from your tickle file and research. It is quite possible you'll get more contacts right over the phone.

Today's Tasks

- Make your *minimum* twenty calls.
- Follow up with people you didn't reach earlier this week.
- Establish dates for follow-up with today's contacts. (Send letters and résumés on those dates.)
- Call associations to get directories. Try to get information over the phone on industry trends or answers to questions you may have. Pump for contacts! Who in the association are consummate networkers? Who are the people that like to talk?
- Don't neglect social contacts. Join clubs—from bridge to square dancing!

Today's Tickle

You faxers, keep tickling!

Today's Review

- What associations or clubs did you join?
- When is the next association meeting?
- When's the next seminar or event? (Often you don't have to be a member to attend.)
- The week's up. Did you reach all one hundred contacts?

Today's Emotional Check

- Isn't it better to be talking to people than sitting there and doing nothing?
- Be prepared for ups and downs.

Today's True Story

Warren was a member of several associations. He used their directories constantly and called members, even if he didn't know them. His specialty was forming strategic alliances for biotech companies.

He found three job openings through networking. Members gave him the names to call inside companies for people who might be able to use his services. He used members' names as references. Warren is back to work and doing exactly what he likes to do.

Next Week

You will begin setting up face-to-face meetings, do more research, and follow up on tickling—expanding your base.

You are almost 17 percent on your way to finding the job you want.

WEEK TWO

Pick Dream Companies or Places of Work

Set Up Informational Meetings

Begin "Tickle" Process

DAY 6

Good morning!

Today's Quote

Nothing will sustain you more potently than the power to recognize in your humdrum routine, as perhaps it may be thought, the true poetry of life—the poetry of the commonplace, of the ordinary man, of the plain, toil-worn woman, with their loves and their joys, their sorrows and their griefs.
—Harvey Cushing

Today's Focus

We will scan general business publications for:

- information on companies
- industries
- trends
- personnel changes
- merger acquisitions
- new products

Try *Forbes, Inc., Barron's, Fortune, Business Week, Newsweek, Time.*

Today's Helpful Hint

Always start networking as high in the organization as possible. These people have the authority and the ability to create jobs and to influence lower levels to do the same.

If contacts are not in, obtain the date they will return and establish a time to call. Place this card in the appropriate tickle-date pocket.

Today's Goals

- Keep increasing your contact list for both new and follow-up calls.
- Begin to research in more depth those companies or places of work that are of interest to you.
- Keep current on the news.
- Reward yourself.

Today's Tasks

- Make copies of pertinent articles and facts from magazines.
- Make at least ten calls from your base list. Follow up with résumé and letter.
- Update your tickle file with today's contacts.
- Begin to prioritize your new contacts with *who* is especially important or helpful and those individuals who you don't want to forget you.
- As potential hidden jobs begin to appear, use informational contacts to find out more about the company or place of work.
- Attend or plan to attend a meeting with some club or association related to your line of work.

Today's Tickle

By today's date, you should have a minimum of ten people you are getting back to, people who have your résumé and who will provide you with two more people whom you can call. Make sure you can use your contact's name as a referral.

Today's Review

- Did you run out of money at the library?
- What did you learn?
- Did your magazine research turn up new contacts?

Today's Emotional Check

Reward: Take forty-five minutes off. Go into the bedroom, close the blinds, loosen your clothes, and lie down. Don't let anyone disturb you. Plan a fantasy vacation—no expenses spared. Visualize yourself there, under a palm tree taking a snooze or at the top of the Matterhorn. The world is yours! Then begin the process of getting there, packing a new wardrobe, selecting the hotel (or tent)! Can you taste the food? Smell the air?

If you find this exercise difficult to do, then while you are lying down, eyes closed, list the ten places you would most like to visit for the first time or go back to. That may get you started on your journey!

Today's True Story

Helen was looking for work in the catalogue business. Her experience was in finding merchandise—unique items for the boudoir. In a tightly closed world, competitive and private, it was too hard to find the Hidden Job Market. She decided to order the entire twelve back issues of *Catalog Age* magazine. She was able to locate a new business start-up and learned enough to present herself and her services to get a job with this start-up.

Tomorrow

More research! Specific industry publications.

DAY 7

Good morning!

Today's Quote

> *No man is born into the world whose work*
> *Is not born with him; there is always work,*
> *And tools to work withal, for those who will;*
> *And blessed are the rough hands of toil!*
> —James Russell Lowell

Today's Focus

Continue your in-depth research by focusing on publications and periodicals about your industry.

There will be general business publications and industry-specific publications. One of your personal contacts should be a friend in an ad agency or a PR firm, so you can get access to a directory called SRDS. It contains information on virtually every business magazine published. With this book you can be sure that you will know about all pertinent publications and where to get them.

Today's Helpful Hint

Don't lower your standards from your Number-One Job Goal.

Today's Goals

- Be familiar with publications in your field. Use them to locate:
    - appropriate companies
    - contacts
    - trends
    - personnel changes
    - mergers/acquisitions
    - general news
- Make your minimum twenty calls.

Today's Tasks

- Copy important features from magazines.
- Make enough calls from your base list. Follow up with résumé and letters, so that you can meet the minimum of twenty (including tickle calls).
- Update tickle file.
- Continue to prioritize your new contacts according to who is especially helpful.

Today's Tickle

Priority: Follow up on all tickles you have.

Today's Review

- What have you learned that's new and important about your industry?
- Can you list ten new companies to contact?
- Are you getting your letters and résumés out on a timely basis (that is, the day you call)?

Today's Emotional Check

- Are you having trouble keeping organized?
- Are you beginning to find that this is driving you nuts?
- Are you feeling isolated?

Today's True Story

Dan was driving in his boss's car from a construction site. The car phone rang. A loyal friend back at the office warned Dan that when he got back to the office, he would be let go because of a cancellation in a project. Dan moved fast!

Dan immediately dialed a friend in the local construction business, who call *his* friend, and so on. Dan took the long way back to the office, and by the time he parked the car, he had work the next day.

Tomorrow

- You'll pick your Ten Dream Companies.
- You'll call for an annual report if it is a public company, or call as if you are a customer, to get information. Try to obtain as much written material as possible.

DAY 8

Good morning!

Today's Quote

The advantage of doing one's praising for oneself is that one can lay it on so thick and exactly in the right places.
—Samual Butler

Today's Focus

We're going to encourage you to dream about your ideal places of employment. We'll use your research to find facts and details to help you in your decision.

We're also going to get you out of the house and in contact with people face to face.

Today's Helpful Hint

Check out the situation in your chosen geographical area—for example, climate, cost of living, schools.

Today's Goals

- From your research, list the Ten Dream Companies you'd like to work at and find out everything you can about them.
- Keep the steam going on your contacts. Make the twenty contacts you most want to build your tickle file.

- Get out of isolation. Practice talking about your strengths and goals. Going to lunch with a friend is a good start.

Today's Tasks

- Identify your Ten Dream Companies. Phone for information.
    - sales information
    - product listings
    - annual report
    - newsletter
- Call a friend for lunch. Make the date for today if possible—if not, then this week.
- Make calls. Most of your original base list has been used. You're using Referent Power from initial contacts and the names they provided you with.

Today's Tickle

You should have at least ten names for follow up.

Today's Review

- What are your Ten Dream Companies?
- When are you having lunch? What are you going to talk about at lunch?
- Is your tickle file working?
- Are you making contact with potential Gatekeepers yet?

Today's Emotional Check

- Does it feel good that you're going to get out?
- Do you dream about this process? If so, do you have good dreams or bad dreams?

Today's True Story

Money in the Bank

Frank was "right-sized" (I hate this expression) out of the accounting department at a large commercial bank. He wisely decided to network through all his old bank customers by first calling and then making personal visits. He soon found that one of his customers was quietly looking for a new comptroller. They knew his work and they knew him. They were *delighted* to hire him!

Tomorrow

It's time to move into informational meetings.

DAY 9

Good morning!

Today's Quote

Man, unlike any other thing organic or inorganic in the universe, grows beyond his work, walks up the stairs of his concepts, emerges ahead of his accomplishments.
—John Steinbeck

Today's Focus

You've now done a lot of research. You're getting a lot of secondary referrals. You've targeted key places to work. You're in the swing of networking. It's time to have informational meetings with key people in your industry.

If you're doing a national search, many of these meetings will be over the phone. Be sure that you've filled any holes in your research and newest business trends (are they regional?). Which companies are up and coming? Which companies do you think are in need of your talents?

Today's Helpful Hint

When you call to make an informational interview, indicate that it will be short—either a quick lunch on you or a twenty-minute meeting. Have your questions ready.

Be prepared to *listen* and then don't be surprised if the meeting lasts longer!

Today's Goals

- Begin to set up informational meetings (you should have one a day—and keep in mind that some will be over the phone) until the end of the fourth week.
- Be sure you're doing twenty contacts a day. The quality of the contacts should be improving daily.

Today's Tasks

- Set up informational meetings for today and tomorrow. You're going to have to plan your meetings ahead of time with the most senior people. You should be setting them up for next week as well.
- Calls to new contacts with follow-up letter and résumé to round out tickle-file contacts.
- Water plant. (*Just testing to see if you're awake!*)
- Send thank-you notes to informational contacts you've had meetings with. Send them that day. Handwritten notes can be personal and effective.

Today's Tickle

You should have at least ten names for follow-up.

Today's Review

- Did you get some informational meetings set up? Are they with key people?
- Are you prepared for the meeting? Can you keep it short?
- Did you write thank-you notes?
- How's your plant? (*Just checking!*)

Today's Emotional Check

- Are you taking care of yourself? How about a hair-cut or a facial? *Something* to make you look and feel better.
- Did it feel good to get dressed up? If you haven't had an informational meeting yet, you have something to look forward to!

Today's True Story

Networking Is in Vogue

Luke is a top fashion art director in New York City. He has been in and out of work more times than he cares to remember. Luckily, he never left the Hidden Job Market for long. In fact, he had one contact, the director of advertising for High Fashion Patterns Company, whom he had kept in touch with for fifteen years, being careful never to put him on the spot by asking him for a job but occasionally asking his advice and opinion. Sure enough, Luke found himself out of work in the deepest recession and quite desperate to find work. He called his friend at High Fashion Patterns and pitched him in earnest. He was hired within the week!

Tomorrow

More meetings.

DAY 10

Good morning!

Today's Quote

> *If one advances confidently in the direction of his dreams, and endeavors to live the life which he has imagined, he will meet with a success unexpected in common hours.*
> —Henry David Thoreau

Today's Focus

- Setting up informational meetings for next week.
- Setting up a social event for weekend.

Today's Helpful Hint

Using another person (Referent Power), an association, or another meaningful link will increase the percentage of getting your calls returned.

Today's Goals

- Keep setting up informational meetings.
- Target at least two Gatekeepers for next week.
- Remember, companies, suppliers, and customers can also be good for informational meetings.
- Be sure to get some fun in your life this weekend.
- Twenty contacts (but you knew that!)

Today's Tasks

- Set up times for informational meetings.
- Make calls to new contacts, followed with letters and résumés to round out tickle-file follow-up.
- Do thank-you notes for face-to-face meetings.
- Go out and buy food for party.

Today's Tickle

You *should* have plenty of names for follow-up.

Today's Review

- Are you ready to party?
- Did you get those meetings set up and scheduled?
- Are your thank-you notes done?
- Do a lot of people know you are out of work?

Today's Emotional Check

- Are you tired?
- How are other people you know who are also out of work doing? Isn't it time to get together with them and share stories?

Today's True Story

What You Don't Know Can Hurt You

That's what Marcy told her network after she was out of a job as head of personnel at a local college. Marcy knew it would be really tough to find another college personnel job. So her strategy was to put her time into developing a phone/in-person survey for local businesses to see if they understood the thorny Equal Employment

Opportunity guidelines. Businesses were usually happy to have an expert evaluate them for free—that is, until one business realized there were many other issues they needed help on, and that they would like Marcy to be their *paid* consultant. Many more businesses eventually put Marcy on board as their expert consultant!

Next Week

You will focus on Gatekeepers. As you know, a Gate-keeper is someone who has the power to hire you.

WEEK THREE

Send Out Extra Information to Contacts

Research Dream Companies, Contact Gatekeepers

Enlarge Dream Company List

DAY 11

Good morning!

Today's Quote

Every man's work, whether it be literature or music or pictures or architecture or anything else, is always a portrait of himself.
—Samuel Butler

Today's Focus

Continue to pursue your Gatekeepers. Send along with the résumé an interesting and current general business article that acts as part of the conversation when we follow up—for example,

- an article from the *Harvard Business Review* related to their industry
- a survey of their customers' habits
- Total Quality Process, strategic intent, Japan versus U.S., environmental issues and Faith Popcorntype trend analysis* are a *few* examples of the information Gatekeepers like. If your Gatekeepers are production oriented or technically oriented, there are many appropriate journals in these fields to consult.

---

*Faith Popcorn, *The Popcorn Report* (New York: Doubleday, 1991).

Today's Helpful Hint

Overnight mail does get attention, but use it sparingly.

Today's Goals

- To enhance your image with potential Gate-keepers and to stand out in the crowd, send an "extra" with your résumé that shows your interest and knowledge of the industry. It's okay if the article has been in a widely read paper, like the *Wall Street Journal*, or a local paper, and you think the person has already seen it. Send it anyhow; you'll get the desired appreciation. You might find a survey that supports you and your skills—as, for instance, if you are from a French family and the results of a survey show that the best chefs come from a French-American background.

Today's Tasks

- Find and copy articles (you may have some in your files). Be sure they are neat and clean copies!
- Send the articles out with letters and résumés to those individuals who are Gatekeepers or influential in the hiring process.
- Make sure you mention, in your phone calls or meetings, that you are going to send them this article—it will increase your chances of being remembered.
- Keep going with *at least* twenty calls—most from the tickle file.
- Information meeting today?

Today's Tickle

Have you collected information about your Ten Dream Companies?

Today's Review

- Have you found, copied, and sent out that general business article, in addition to having extra copies on hand for future mailings?
- Have you caught up with your contacts?

Today's Emotional Check

- Are you getting any exercise? Go out and play!
- Are you nervous when you talk to Gatekeepers?
- Is your nervousness preventing your confidence from shining through?

Today's True Story

Seeing Is Believing in the Hidden Job Market

Nancy, who had a Ph.D. in engineering, specializing in optics, was out of a job when the small eyeglass lens factory where she worked went bankrupt, but now she was free to follow her dream: to work at one of the world's largest optics company. Confidently, she replied to an ad that was *written for her!* Nothing happened. Nothing was *going to happen!*

So, Nancy learned how to network into her dream company using the Hidden Job Market, beginning with one friend who referred her to another. Her goal was to find out who the manager was that had advertised the opening she had read about. Once she did, she wrote to him directly with a personal letter that included her references. The next day, she was invited for an interview and yes, you guessed it, she got the job!

Tomorrow

Dream Company follow-up date.

DAY 12

Good morning!

Today's Quote

> *Though little, I'll work as hard as a Turk,*
> *If you'll give me employ,*
> *To plow and sow, and reap and mow,*
> *And be a farmer's boy.*
> —Anonymous

Today's Focus

Dream Company follow-up: time to start getting you introduced to the Gatekeepers.

Time to generate your list of the *next* Ten Dream Companies.

Today's Helpful Hint

Use your library's microfiche film index to periodicals to access information, past and present, on Dream Companies.

See if you can locate in business libraries Dow Jones, Dialog, and other on-line information systems. You could ask a friend or new contact to do this for you or to help, and this person may be able to help you get information on your Dream Companies in other ways, too!

Today's Goals

- Get through the day. Heard a good joke lately? Watch the Comedy Channel.
- Become very familiar with your Ten Dream Companies. Your ten *new* companies: Do they fit your criteria—for example, in such areas as geography, industry, personality and philosophy, training, opportunity for growth?
- Why are your Dream Companies your Dream Companies?
- Keep on top of *minimum* twenty calls.

Today's Tasks

- Continue informational interviews.
- Make sure you are making your calls.
- Include articles with résumé when it seems appropriate.
- Contact your Ten Dream Companies today. Your network should have helped you identify key contacts and referred you to them. If not, your research could be a good starting point.

Today's Tickle

See Today's Tasks.

Today's Review

- How did the contacts with your Dream Companies go? Have you identified Gatekeepers?
- Are you continuing your informational interviews and getting more quality contacts?
- Are you keeping up with correspondence?

Today's Emotional Check

- What have been the emotional highs and lows for the past week? How are you handling these highs and lows?
- Are you getting support from family and friends?

Today's True Story

Mike was marketing for a chemical company. Because of a reduction in the work force, he was let go. He heard, through networking, that there was an opening in his Dream Company. He located the Gatekeeper and said he was going to sit in the lobby until the guy would see him.

He came, very politely, and sat there for about three days. Finally, he met with the Gatekeeper and they talked about the job. Mike then said, "I'm going to sit here until you hire me." Although not a tactic one wants to regularly use, it does show that persistence pays off. He got the job!

Tomorrow

- Finish up Ten Dream Companies.
- Complete research on next ten.

DAY 13

Good morning!

Today's Quote

I don't like work—no man does—but I like what is in work—the chance to find yourself. Your own reality—for yourself, not for others—what no other man can ever know.
—Joseph Conrad

Today's Focus

Today you are increasing your total Dream Company effort to thirty companies.

- First ten
- Second ten
- Ten small companies

You need to continue your momentum with informational meetings.

Today's Helpful Hint

If you are calling a company without Referent Power, call the secretary to the president. *Be nice:* you don't mean to take *her* time, but could she please refer you to the vice president of manufacturing (or whoever the Gatekeeper is) so that you could get some information?

Call his office, explain that you were referred by Mary Jones (the president's secretary) and that she felt that he would be an appropriate person to talk to. Is he in?

"What's this all about?" "I'm a member of XY Association and I need to speak to him" OR "It's about what's happening in the industry and Ms. Jones felt he could speak for the company."

Well, that's *one* creative approach. Remember, you're not asking for a job!

Today's Goals

- Rounding up Dream Company Gatekeepers you missed yesterday.
- Finishing the gathering and processing of information on your second Ten Dream Companies.
- Focusing on ten smaller Dream Companies (fifty employees or less).

Today's Tasks

- Make calls. Get to those Gatekeepers!
- Identify Gatekeepers for second Ten Dream Companies.
- Compile list of ten small companies.
- Be sure to meet today. Lunch? Breakfast?
- Do your everyday twenty contacts. Remember quick follow-ups with letters, résumé, and articles.

Today's Tickle

It's probably time to take a few minutes to check that you remain organized and that your tickle file hasn't become a graveyard.

Today's Review

- Who haven't you reached in your Dream Company?

- Were you out of the office today meeting people?
- Do you have a hint of at least one potential job opening? If it fits your criteria, go for it!

Today's Emotional Check

- How is all of this affecting your love life?
- Are you over the *visible* anger of losing your job?
- Is the anticipation of being in your ideal job beginning to surface?
- Do you feel more in command?

Today's True Story

The Clam That Wasn't Half-Baked

Janet wanted to help her husband find a job. The billing department, where he had worked for over twenty-seven years, was abolished as his employer merged with another large firm. Jim hadn't the vaguest idea of how to network, and anyway, he wasn't in much shape emotionally to talk to anyone about his future.

Well, Janet threw a huge clambake, a virtual "net" to find work. The local truck-stop owner was there, crying in his beer. He didn't have enough reliable help, nor was there anyone locally with the accounting experience he needed, and so on.

Meanwhile, Jim was crying in his beer too, and he shared his story. Well, blame it on the beer or whatever, but despite himself Jim was presented with a job offer that very afternoon!

Tomorrow

Finish contacting the second Ten Dream Companies and start contacting the ten smaller companies.

DAY 14

Good morning!

Today's Quote

> *An open hand,*
> *and easy shoe,*
> *and a hope to make*
> *the day go through.*
> —Owen Wister

Today's Focus

We are moving toward completion of contacting the Thirty Dream Companies.

Today's Helpful Hint

Do not rule out organizations that just had big layoffs or early retirement incentives. They often backfill with people in specialized skills.

Today's Goals

- Finish second Ten Dream Companies list and start contracting small-company Gatekeepers.
- Start winding down informational meetings, because we will begin to focus on issues around job interviewing and getting the Gatekeeper on your side.

Today's Tasks

- Maintain twenty contacts, set follow-up dates, and move to tickle date (what you have been doing so well all along).
- Squeeze in as many informational meetings as possible.
- Call contacts on second list of Ten Dream Companies you have not been able to reach. Talk to them!
- Keep up on the news. General *and* business.

Today's Tickle

Don't laugh. Keeping following up—promptly!

Today's Review

- Are you anticipating difference responses from smaller companies?
- Will you have to adjust your résumé? How will you present your skills?
- Have you had enough informational meetings to give you the self-confidence you'll need for interviewing?
- Are you confident there is work in your industry?

Today's Emotional Check

- Are you gaining confidence in this process?
- Do you feel at the mercy of the Gatekeepers? What might change that?
- Bet you're surprised at how helpful people have been!

Today's True Story

Meet the Silver Fox

Richard Fox was the CEO of a large electronics company in Detroit. He was forced out by a man twenty-five years his junior. Richard carefully focused his trip into the Hidden Job Market. He decided to go where business was booming—Silicon Valley. He chose to network through the companies that were his competitors in the past. He narrowed the field to those who could use an "old fox" because they were in some sort of desperate business situation and needed his experience. He and a company that really needed help in turning around to become profitable found each other in—you guessed it!—thirty days!

Tomorrow

- Complete all informational interviews.
- Complete dream contacts for small companies.

DAY 15

Good morning!

Today's Quote

> *Blessed is he who has found his work;*
> *let him ask no other blessedness.*
> —Thomas Carlyle

Today's Focus

This week brings an end to our major effort in informational meetings, casual lunches, and Dream Company contacts.

To summarize, you should have made over three hundred contacts and have had *at least* ten informational meetings. You should have identified key Gatekeepers (but we're not done with that!), and should know your business up and down.

You should have a smooth working office. You are well along in the process.

Halfway! Way to go!

Today's Helpful Hint

Even most of the worst-hit industries for jobs are hiring; that includes retail, real estate, advertising, and publishing. Look in their publications. People are moving—in the Hidden Job Market, that is!

Today's Goals

Last calls and informational business meetings today:

- to Dream Companies for information
- your daily twenty *minimum* contacts continue

Today's Tasks

- Make calls. Follow up.
- Review office procedures. Fix glitches today. Running low on résumés?
- Filing sorted out?
- Give somebody a hug.

Today's Tickle

Review how last three weeks have gone for any tips or clues on improving procedures. Think back to where you were three weeks ago and look at where you are today!

Today's Review

- How many opportunities can you smell out there?
- Out of your Thirty Dream Companies, what do you think your hit rate will be?
- Have you been keeping up with your regular twenty contacts?

Today's Emotional Check

- Don't you feel you have a lot to offer?
- Don't you look forward to the time you'll turn down a job offer because you have a better one?
- Family still on your side?
- What puts a smile on your face?

Today's True Story

"I Wanted the Job So Much I Bought the Company!"

Gary felt his long life in the printing trade was over when he was forced out as CEO of a large printing company. He did have a ready list of contacts, and he soon found a printing company that was looking for a vice president of sales. Although told he was overqualified, he saw a tremendous opportunity for this company's growth. Gary went back to his network, got a consortium together, and bought the company!

Next Week

Focus on the BIG PUSH into the Hidden Job Market— directly through the gate.

WEEK FOUR

Move in on the Gatekeepers

Maintain Contact Process

Update Your Knowledge of Your Occupation

Prepare to be Very Articulate About How Your
Expertise Is Important *and* Valuable

DAY 16

Good morning!

Today's Quote

This job strategy accounts for 70 percent of all the jobs our career counseling continuation clients accept. The job seeker constructs a network by talking to friends and business acquaintances who introduce him or her to a continually expanding circle of personal contacts. We've watched thousands of individuals get good new jobs by building networks that expand through the business universe until they find jobs they have been seeking. It sounds mysterious, but it isn't.
—William J. Morin, Chairman of Drake Beam Morin, Inc.

Today's Focus

Don't give up! All your hard work will start to pay off. Your experience on the phone and informational meetings has put you in an excellent position to make this the most productive week so far.

The stress this week will be placed on getting your thoughts and questions together so that you come off well with the Gatekeepers. Now is when the industry research you've done for the last few weeks gives you the momentum and knowledge base that separates you from the crowd.

Today's Helpful Hint

Be able to express your knowledge about your business in your *own* words. Don't just mouth what you've read.

Today's Goals

- Your experience with your network should provide this week's contacts and more Gatekeepers.
- Organize industry information so that you can articulate on most issues in your business.

Today's Tasks

- Make your twenty contacts. Get those Gatekeeper names. *Do* follow up.
- Contact your Dream Companies at the Gatekeeper level.
- Review *at least* ten articles a day from your research. Be sure you know and understand the topics. If you read that your Dream Company has just gotten a new customer, for example, find out all about the customer and the future potential for your Dream Company.

Today's Tickle

Start being qualitative about your contacts.

Today's Review

- Compare today's contacts with last week's. Are you making progress?
- What do you think the top five issues in your business are today?
- Have you learned that any of your Dream Companies aren't as dreamy as you thought?

Today's Emotional Check

- Are you concerned about the kind of job atmosphere you may find at your new job?
- Are you trying to find places you'll *fit in?*
- Think about something *good* that happened today!

Today's True Story

Debbie dreamed about working at an advertising agency. She was a recent grad with a great portfolio, but no agency wanted to hire someone so junior. She decided to get advice—*informational interviews*—from the major clients who belonged to an agency she really wanted to work at. Clients gave her lots of advice and made her very savvy about what agencies should do to make clients happy! Finally, a generous client realized her potential, and then another! They gave her general letters of reference to take to agencies. Guess how fast the agency hired her!

Tomorrow

A Gatekeeper contact day. A focused thrust into companies you want to work for.

DAY 17

Good morning!

Today's Quote

> *I like the dreams of the future better than the*
> *history of the past.*
> —Thomas Jefferson

Today's Focus

Gatekeepers. Get in front of them as much as you can from now on. Use the phone when you need to; get in front of them any way you can. They need to *know* you.

Back to your research file.

Today's Helpful Hint

In job hunting, familiarity does *not* breed contempt. It spawns offers.

Today's Goals

- Get to know three *new* Gatekeepers.
- Summarize more industry articles.

Today's Tasks

- Continue your twenty contacts.
- We haven't reminded you in a while, but be sure you are promptly following up with letters. If you don't know this routine by now, it's too late!

- Call enough Gatekeepers to get three solid new meetings (or lunch), if possible.
- Do your daily follow-up.
- Finish the second batch of articles you collected during your research.

Today's Tickle

Go *back* through the days. See if any quality leads still need following up. Take time to catch up!

Today's Review

- Is your research sparking any interest in the Gatekeepers?
- Have you gotten the impression in any of your conversations that you know more than the person you are talking to?
- Do you feel as though you're close to getting an interview for a real job?

Today's Emotional Check

In talking to your contacts, have you sensed anybody that you really click with? Put this person's card aside. Use your senses; you're going to be able to use chemistry to your advantage.

Today's True Story

Betsy took her seat in the first-class cabin (using her frequent-flyer upgrade) of a jet leaving New York for Los Angeles. As the jet was waiting on the runway, Betsy felt a tap on her shoulder. A very famous and gorgeous blond TV star whispered to her, "Please come sit next to me. This guy is bothering me." Betsy moved next to the star and she shooed away the boorish guy.

Betsy, a freelance script writer, used this opportunity for Reference Power. By the end of the flight, the grateful star had practically given Betsy her personal phone book. Thanks to this flight, Betsy got her big break for a prime-time show script!

Tomorrow

You've got to start tackling communicating with Gate-keepers. You don't want to be caught unprepared by a surprise interview or meeting offer.

DAY 18

Good morning!

Today's Quote

> *Work only half a day. It makes no difference which half—the first 12 hours or the last 12 hours.*
> —Kemmons Wilson

Today's Focus

Digging deep into our Gatekeeper group. Hanging in there. Not giving up. Dealing with discouragement. Getting ready to "walk the talk."

Today's Helpful Hint

When you're making a call, here's some important advice from a super salesperson:

What do you think of this as an opening remark from a salesperson on a call? "Mr. Prospect, my company is in business to make a profit, and if you buy some of our products, it will help us to reach out profit objectives for this year."

Ridiculous, isn't it? You would never say that. But often salespeople say something like that non-verbally with their manner, with an outward expression of an inner concern. Communications experts have been telling us for years that the overwhelming effect of communication is nonverbal. It's not the words but the feelings that are being transmitted. Ralph Waldo Emerson put it eloquently when he said, "What you are stands over you . . . and thunders so that I cannot hear what you say to the contrary."

To say this is not to diminish the importance of goal setting. In selling, goals must be confined to the planning stages. But when you are in contact with prospects, their goals take number-one priority.   The only way you can satisfy your goals is to satisfy theirs.

1. People do things for their reasons, not yours.
2. Prospects are not much interested in your products or services. They are interested only in what your products or services will *do* for them.

—Lee Boyan, *Successful Cold Call Selling*

Today's Goals

- Call twenty contacts, as usual.
- Assess strengths and weakness of your work so far. Are you having trouble keeping up with the number of contacts every day?

Today's Tasks

- Be sure you reach those three new Gatekeepers. Be sure they know your special strengths.
- Note on 3 x 5 cards the information you want to "tuck away" in your memory book to use on an interview. What did you *learn* from the Gatekeeper?
- Call twenty contacts. Follow up with letter and

résumé. Remember, you are trying to "trade up" the management ladder.

Today's Tickle

So who y'gonna call?

Today's Review

- Did you find a second article, a general business article, to send with your letters and résumé?
- Are you *knowledgeable* about your business? Up to date? Fabulously articulate?
- What obstacles, in the process, have you reached?

Today's Emotional Check

- Tired? Overwhelmed? That's okay. You're working, you're doing it!
- Is anything holding you back?
- This is "hump" week (after this week, you're over the hump). Keep plowing.

Today's True Story

Jim was a tool designer and mechanical engineer whose small-town tool company went out of business. Doing his research, Jim came across an aviation magazine (he liked flying) and noticed an item about a small airline that was planning to establish a repair depot. He jumped in his car and drove the hour to visit the place. He talked with an engineer there and learned about the plans for the machine shop. Using the engineer for Referent Power, he called the Gatekeeper, the manager. Jim gave his résumé over the phone and went even further, suggesting that the airline could make money repairing trucks and other machines and that he could find all the necessary tools (they were sitting in his old shop).

Well, Jim found himself a terrific job!

Tomorrow

Reality check.

DAY 19

Good morning!

Today's Quote

> *If I keep a green bough in my heart, the singing bird will come.*
> —Chinese proverb

Today's Focus

Who is left in your Dream Companies for you to contact? Let's go over, through, or under the brick walls you've hit.

Could you handle an interview, if you haven't handled one already? Present yourself as a candidate who can fill *needs,* who can contribute extra knowledge or a willingness to learn (whatever is your case)? Do you have your skills prioritized to the Gatekeeper's needs?

Today's Helpful Hint

Don't forget Standard & Poor's Corporation's *Register of Corporations, Directors and Executives.* Review it for top Gatekeepers.

Also, there may be some important social contacts you need to follow up with. Keep your mind open. Call up those long-forgotten college friends. Use your school alumni association.

Today's Goals

- Twenty contacts. Keep 'em alive.
- What do you think is good and bad during this process?

Potential Bad

1. Contacts not giving me two names.
   If you can't get two, you'll take one! Be emphatic when you call back. Even one could make a difference.

2. Contacts never in.
   Be sure you learn when they will be back. Try before and after work.

3. Letters and resumés not going out same day.
   Slow typing? A lot of time out of the office? Do letters after dinner!

4. Lots of contacts, but not leading to interviews.
   Remember, you are doing your best to be first in line for an opening but you may not be controlling the timing. Are you going high enough! Are people turned off before they know about you? Are you pushing for a job when, really, all you want is advice?

Potential Good

1. Lots of new friends in lots of places of work.
   Your tickle is working. So are your selections for your contact list.

2. You feel competent and comfortable Positioning You. Pitching You has become (and will) get smoother.

3. You can *smell* a job out there in the Hidden Job Market. Yes, there is work—your work to be found.

Today's Tasks

- Make your twenty calls. Follow up. File.
- Be sure you make plenty of copies of your article. Rewrite your cover letter, if you think it would help explain your choice of this article.

  In light of today's recession, I thought this article on the latest California Census Analysis would help explain why today's car buyers are becoming older demographically. [This could be from you if you're in the auto business.]

- Be extra careful on the phone. Keep your charming manners. Practice your please and thank-yous.

Today's Tickle

Who's stopping you at your Dream Company? Well, find out who *their* boss is (or better yet, the boss over *that* boss) and put him or her on your 3 x 5 card. See if you can use Referent Power to get to him or her. If not, make an informational call for advice.

Today's Review

- Did you resolve your good and bad experiences so far?
- Have you made your twenty calls?

Today's Emotional Check

BE BOLD! The whole trick, as I said at the beginning of this book, is to be Pro-Active, not Re-Active.

Today's True Story

Bob was looking for work in his specialty: fundraising for nonprofits. He went to get his blood pressure checked at a mobile medical center (a van from a local hospital). The doctor in the van told him that he would have to find another place, from now on, to get his blood pressure checked, since funds for the mobile medical center had been reallocated. Bob talked at length with the doctor and got his permission to use his name at the hospital as a reference for an informational interview.

The hospital told Bob they had never had a grants administrator, as Bob described himself, at the hospital. Well, Bob got hired on a trial basis and quickly raised the money not only for his salary but for the mobile medical center and many other projects as well.

Tomorrow

More Gatekeeper contact.

DAY 20

Good morning!

Today's Quote

I don't want to offer them [American workers] comfort. I want to offer them jobs. We've got to build jobs.
—Lee Iacocca

Today's Focus

How good are you at getting to Gatekeepers? Don't try to force a meeting—even on the phone you can get their help, advice, and Referent Power.

Keep these Gatekeepers alive by promising that you will stay in touch (do so with articles and news items that you think will be interesting and, naturally, your résumé).

Today's Helpful Hint

Check out *Who's Who in America* and the *Reference Book of Corporate Management* (Dun & Bradstreet). Go through your library's microfilm data. You will be surprised at the possible Referent Power you can find when you see the clubs this person belongs to, where he or she went to school, and so on.

Today's Goals

- Your daily twenty contacts, including the Gate-keepers who will hear from you!

Today's Tasks

- Review your stock of office supply and make list of supplies to buy for Monday.
- Visit library to see new trade publications. Clip VIP items and copy.
- Make your twenty calls. Are you finding your résumé needs to be customized to fit potential job needs and problems you can solve? Now is the time to quickly get any new versions printed if you feel they would sell you better.

Today's Tickle

Sift through today's tickle file. Which contacts are truly *not* close to your Number-One Job Goal? You have to edit your contacts and weed out the less pertinent ones. By now you should have the Referent Power of several hundred people in the Hidden Job Market.

Today's Review

Did you find a hot news item to send to the gatekeepers for your Number-One Job Goal?

Have you talked with gatekeepers who you believe are decision makers in the Hidden Job Market?

Today's Emotional Check

- Do you have plenty of energy and enthusiasm today?
- Are you ready for a weekend of rest and fun?
- Are you over your fear of rejection?

Today's True Story

Sammy, a system analyst for a large computer manufacturing and distribution company, was trapped in a
massive "restructuring." On the pink-slip day, he told
his family he was too disappointed to go on their regular
bowling league night. However, his kids insisted and
dragged him to the bowling alley anyway. The team
captain wanted to know why Sammy looked so glum
(and was bowling so badly). Gathering his ego (he was
still in shock and thought he was not ready to tell
anyone), he confessed what had happened. The captain's
eyes lit up. "Sammy," he said, "with your experience
with Federal agencies, your availability, and your training, you could help us build our new software business."
Sammy was hired! Would that every True Story were
such a fairy tale come true!

Next Week

- You'll get information about successful interviewing.
- We'll get meetings set up and scheduled and go
  deep into the Hidden Job Market to actually find
  job openings.

WEEK FIVE

Practice Interviewing—Focus on *Skills*

Keep Up Steam with Contacts and Follow Up

Set Up Face-to-Face Meetings/Interviews
in Dream Companies

DAY 21

Good morning!

Today's Quote

Over the years, I've evolved a somewhat heretical but time- and mind-saving approach to books, articles, editorials that deal with weighty matters. More often than not, by beginning at the end and contemplating the conclusions, one can determine if it's worth going through the whole to get there.
—Malcolm Forbes

Today's Focus

This week starts another education program. The topic of this effort is the job interview. You may have had an interview already, but probably they will come this week and next. You have already been prepared for meetings with Gatekeepers, but that was for you to get advice from them.

Now you are going to be put on the spot and will have to respond. We will not neglect the traditional networking follow-up and meetings with Gatekeepers, however.

Today's Helpful Hint

Never criticize your present or past employers in front of anyone who could hold a key to a job. Keep that between family, counselors, and very close friends.

Today's Goals

- Develop lists of potential interviewer's questions and answers to those questions.
- Continue to make your *minimum* twenty contacts.
- Sharpen your skills in identifying and contacting people in high places and in discussing subjects with them.

Today's Tasks

- With a group of friends, develop lists of questions that will be asked at interviews. Formulate answers that will survive the rigors of many people's input.
- Make your twenty contacts and follow up.

Today's Tickle

Look back over the informational meetings you had. What were the most-often-asked questions? Are you comfortable with your answers, *now,* to those questions? Do they feel like part of you or were you just mouthing words?

Today's Review

- Does the thought of an interview scare or excite you?
- Would a question you were not expecting cause you to be rattled?
- Do you handle interviews well?

Today's Emotional Check

- Can you maintain this pace for two more weeks?
- Do you really want the sky to open up and a job to appear magically?

- Can you deal with being interviewed and not getting a job offer?

Today's True Story

Bill was in marketing, and for three years he had been working miles away from his wife and family. It was getting old. He sat down with a friend, an editor of a business/technical magazine that was located in the same city as his family. The editor had just gotten a new job and was leaving his old job as editor, and the magazine was looking for someone with Bill's qualifications. He was recommended by his friend for the job and was hired.

Tomorrow

More contacts, and sharpening your interviewing skills.

DAY 22

Good morning!

Today's Quote

There's a tremendous amount of pressure on both sexes, but there's a double pressure on women to compete in the marketplace, to bring home half the salary that's needed, if not the whole salary, and to look beautiful and be slender and all the rest of it. I think we're superheroes.
—Jane Fonda

Today's Focus

- More on interviewing and being prepared.
- More follow-up with contacts (all high-level by now or maybe one level lower).
- Contact people who do job interviews for a living and friends that have just gone through some interviews.

Today's Helpful Hint

Keep answers short. Don't anticipate. Try to illustrate answers to questions by using a short example. It shows you have experience and it makes you memorable to the interviewer.

Today's Goals

- Gain more experience about interviewing from people you know.
- Continue to focus your efforts on gaining more high-level contacts. Use your instincts now—they should be developing.
- Make as many face-to-face contacts as you can.

Today's Tasks

- Through your networking, you should have found someone who is part of a human resources department or a psychological testing service or someone who has a lot of experience interviewing. Now is the time to pump this person on every aspect of the interview process.
- Make appointments with friends and contacts who have been interviewed. Get their suggestions. Many people who have outplacement as part of their package have access to questions and answers. Talk to them.
- Make your twenty contacts. Don't stop now!

Today's Tickle

Were there any contacts at your Dream Companies who could help you with the interview process?

Today's Review

Have you had an interview? Do you have one scheduled? How did it go? What would you do differently? Can you believe that four weeks ago interviews seemed so far away?

Today's Emotional Check

- If you don't have an interview scheduled, don't be discouraged. One will come your way *soon.*
- What's the best thing that has happened so far in the process? Can you capitalize on that?

Today's True Story

Joe is a high flyer, a man on the rise. He has worked with many top executives. No task was too small, no job too difficult. Joe has never been out of work. He has been pulled by executive after executive into new opportunities. Even if Joe does fall on hard times, he will always have a job. Why? Is he good? Yes! Is he bright and personable? Yes! Does he network? Constantly! He is at his *best* when he is networking!

Tomorrow

More tips on interviewing, more practice, more work.

DAY 23

Good morning!

Today's Quote

> *My interest is in the future because I am going to
> spend the rest of my life there.*
> —Charles F. Kettering

Today's Focus

- We are going to do some reading and consulting
  with experts on interviewing. You will practice
  your responses, make them comfortable for you.
  Do not recite them from memory or tire from
  being asked the same questions. Be fresh, be in
  command.
- Continue to develop your contacts. Gatekeepers
  and people who have inside information are the
  ones who are important.

Today's Helpful Hint

Always maintain eye contact. Be enthusiastic, but *never*
give a salary range or figure when asked. Concentrate on
the job, its attributes, and your desire to have that job.
The last thing *you* want to do is talk about money Let the
interviewer raise the issue. When you find yourself
negotiating—name a figure *at least* 15 percent over your
target. It helps to know what the job would typically pay
before you go into an interview.

Today's Goals

Be in command under fire. You are ready. You know how to handle yourself.

Today's Tasks

- Get and review these books:

Winning the Job Interview Game: Tips for the High Tech Era, by Jo Danna (Palomino Press).

Knock 'Em Dead with Great Answers to Tough Interview Questions, by Martin Yate (Bob Adams, Inc.).

Sweaty Palms: The Neglected Art of Being Interviewed, by H. Anthony Medley (Ten Speed Press).

Your First Interview: Everything You Need to Know to Ace the Interviewing Process and Get Your First Job, by Ron Fry (Career Press).

- Keep networking and make your *minimum* twenty calls.

Today's Tickle

Always follow an interview with letters to *each* of the interviewers. I had a friend who went through some sixteen interviews at one company before she got the job. A lot of work, but it paid off.

Today's Review

- Do you know everything you want to know about interviewing now?
- Are you maintaining your twenty-contact-a-day pace?
- Have you been able to convert your contacts to references that have led to interviews?
- Keep it up!

Today's Emotional Check

- Have your friends continued to help you?

Today's True Story

Mary was a market researcher for a large photographic company. She was excellent at doing focus groups, being a facilitator for meetings. She wanted to go out on her own. The company had a reduction in their work force. Prior to their offering her the opportunity to leave, she set up contacts with key people in the company. She took the separation package and had enough contacts to start her own business. It was networking on the job that allowed her to get started.

Tomorrow

Lights! Camera! Action! Taping you on an interview.

DAY 24

Good morning!

Today's Quote

> *Interviewers probe for illustrations of distinct skills and well-defined accomplishments, the yardsticks for competence in the 1990s. Conventional criteria such as "years of experience" now seem of less value and dubious to many employers.*
>
> *For example: While screening a candidate for a job requiring database research skills, the interviewer might call for specific examples of research assignments that the candidate undertook, a description of how he or she attempted to complete them, and a candid accounting of the results.*
>
> *A response without these details will ruffle an interviewer, who's then likely to dismiss the candidate along with the inadmissible evidence.*
>
> *Because many employers now write job descriptions that include a list of skills in addition to the customary roster of duties, questions that ferret out explicit skills are increasingly fashionable among interviewers, if not mandated.*
>
> —Philip Mulivor

Today's Focus

- It is *extremely* important for you to learn how you come across in front of people. Today we are going to tape you in several interviewing situations.

- Now more than ever, it is important for you to maintain your contacting schedule. You may have had an interview or two and are waiting to hear.
- Don't put yourself in a position where you will have to start over if these interviews don't come through for you—you will be weeks behind if you do. Remember, networking is never over, even after you find a job. Unless you have negotiated and accepted a position, you *must* keep the pedal to the metal.

Today's Helpful Hint

Always ask questions about the company on an interview. Use opened-ended questions that can't be answered with just a yes or no. Target the questions so that you can determine how you can best contribute to the company.

Today's Goals

- Develop skills in front of the camera: Listen to your answers, the tone of your voice. Look at how you are dressed. Would *you* hire you?
- Continue networking. Your hit rate should be at its highest at this point. Strike while you are hot.

Today's Tasks

- Rent or borrow a video camera and set up mock interviews using friends who are professionals. Let the interviewers ask you tough questions, and be serious about your answers.

- Call your twenty contacts and get in front of them. Always test for signs of a job opening (but never ask for one). Always have them suggest further contacts.

Today's Tickle

Look back. You have mastered your industry and are comfortable with Gatekeepers, and the interview process is almost behind you. You're there, right? Wrong! There is more to come next week. You are not there until you have accepted the job.

Today's Review

- How did you do on camera? Isn't it weird hearing and seeing yourself?
- Are you behind in your contacts? Has this activity slipped? If so, get back on track.
- It is too easy to let up now. If you do, the odds will begin to favor someone else. You *can't* let that happen! You *aren't going* to let that happen!

Today's Emotional Check

- Are you able to speak calmly, confidently at an interview or on the phone?
- Feeling nervous? As soon as you do, simply *smile*—it will relax your face. A quick smile keeps you confident—upbeat.

Today's True Story

Sharon was working in industry, but she had always stayed close to her academic roots, thanks to the fact that she had continually cultivated her academic contacts while she was working. Networking *never stops!* Her strength was that she knew her area of scientific endeavor better than most—in fact, she was one of the top three in her field—and industry had used her knowledge. But now times were hard and she was looking for work. The universities needed her prestige, her knowledge. They hired her right away because they knew her and they were building their departments.

Tomorrow

One more day of camera work.

DAY 25

Good morning!

Today's Quote

> *But I, being poor, have only my dreams;*
> *I have spread my dreams under your feet;*
> *Tread softly because you tread on my dreams.*
> —William Butler Yeats

Today's Focus

- Last day in front of the camera. You are now a master interviewee.
- At the end of today, you will have over five hundred contacts. Your tickle file will be jammed into next week. Obviously, not all of the follow-ups and contacts will be completed on the thirtieth day.

Today's Helpful Hint

If you haven't found out by now, interviewers are not perfect. Some people are so unfamiliar with interviewing that you'll end up putting them at ease. (By the way, there are jerks everywhere, but you aren't one of them, and if you run into one, you will handle this person in a professional manner. Don't let anyone bring you down to his or her level.)

Today's Goals

- Finish your on-camera interviews.
- Chalk up your five hundredth contact (at least) today!

Today's Tasks

- This time on camera, have your friends hit you with everything they've got. It is your job to handle it.
- Continue with Gatekeepers, key people, and refining your list of contacts for next week.

Today's Tickle

Have you been keeping special contacts separate from others? Follow up with these people. Stay in touch. Tell them you will continue to contact them even after you get a job.

Today's Review

- Well, you're ready for anything, right?
- No one knows more than you and people are now asking *you* for advice.
- Now you are ready for next week!

Today's Emotional Check

- How are you going to feel when you get the job offer? You may be surprised in more ways than one!
- Of all the people you know who are out of work, who's doing the best emotionally?

Today's True Story

Marge had been very active in her industry association. She had chaired many committees. She represented her company well. She was now a director of the association, but her company was having trouble; she sensed it. Over the years, she had learned to present herself well. She had always been on the business side of bringing out new products, even though she had a technical background. Through networking, she found that the position of technical director was open in a competitor's company. Companies were now looking to make their research-and-development groups more responsible to business needs. She was the candidate of choice because she had networked into the job and helped shape the requirements for the job.

Next Week

Your last week is coming up. Time to negotiate.

WEEK SIX

Be sure you are getting out of the house and
meeting gatekeepers.

Network full speed ahead . . . don't give up now!

Confirm your Number-One Job Goal—
check criteria—is it still realistic?

DAY 26

Good morning!

Today's Quote

For people out of work, networking may well be the most widely recommended way to find a job.
—John Lucht, formerly at Heidrick and Struggles, Inc.

Today's Focus

This is The Week. Your most productive week. You are going after companies, people, and positions you know are meant for you. You may be facing a factor that is not under your control: the actual timing of the job opening. Also, there may be conditions that are not to your liking in a job offer. Remember, there are things you can control and they are separate from things you can't. Your mission is to be a master of what you can control.

Today's Helpful Hint

When you know you are invited back for a second interview, try to find out about your competition. Are there any internal candidates? Where do you stand? See if you can gently learn what the company likes about you and what has put you in the running.

Today's Goals

- Keep in front of Gatekeepers. Recontact people who were part of the interview team. Increase your knowledge and you increase the power of your position.
- Pull out all stops. In your contacts, always go the fastest near the finish. Much is depending on giving this effort your complete attention.
- Think about what aspects of a job offer are negotiable and what are your "sticking points."

Today's Tasks

- List all possible job factors that you can think of:
  - title
  - office space
  - salary
  - perks
  - work hours
  - benefits
  - many, many others
- Prioritize the factors from most interest to least.
- Continue your contacts, follow up. Don't let up.
- If there are any pending contacts, call them today.

Today's Tickle

Any new articles out in the new issues of the magazines, papers, and periodicals you have been following? Your homework never stops!

Today's Review

Why is it a good idea to think about offers before you have one? Simply because a job offer can slip up on you. A second interview could be a job offer, and you may have to handle certain questions before you thought you would. We want you to be ahead of the field, the interviewer, and everyone else. Tired of contacting people? You'll get no sympathy here . . . keep it up!

Today's Emotional Check

- At all costs, do not let the excitement of an offer sweep you into accepting.
- How do you turn down an offer?
- Won't it feel good to have a choice?

Today's True Story

Don't sit around; you're not networking when you're sitting around. Walking dogs was not what Samantha felt was her life's calling, but it gave her exercise, she liked dogs, and it paid the bills. Actually, it paid more than she bargained for. One of her clients offered her a job at his modeling agency—her Number-One Job Goal!

Tomorrow

More constructive thoughts about job offers.

DAY 27

Good morning!

Today's Quote

I used to think as I looked out on the Hollywood night—there must be thousands of girls sitting alone like me, dreaming of becoming a movie star. But I'm not going to worry about them. I'm dreaming the hardest.
—Marilyn Monroe

Today's Focus

- Practice your negotiations with friends. Have them put you in tight spots where you have to make choices. Use some of your best prospects and construct situations you expect to encounter.
- Line up those contacts. Bring in those interviews.

Today's Helpful Hint

We have seen job interviewees be rejected for one job and at the same time be offered another position. Sometimes the offer was weeks later. Don't think a missed job is a missed opportunity.

Today's Goals

- Get your friends together and work on key job factors, negotiations, and your nerves.
- Bring in those interviews and job offers. If you don't believe you are the best candidate for the job, no one else will.

Today's Tasks

- Get your friends over. Set up conditions at five to ten companies and role-play.
- Make your twenty calls and follow up.
- Party with your friends afterward.

Today's Tickle

Look back at your research on places, cost of living, and other factors. Use this work to form the basis for what you are after when negotiations are in full swing.

Today's Review

- How's the role playing?
- Got your priorities straight?

Today's Emotional Check

Can you taste a job yet? Is it hard to stay focused when the end is near?

Today's True Story

Marilyn was an art-market expert and had been out of work for a year. In order to keep her skills current, she took a position as a part-time salesperson at a large city gallery. Within a month, her networking connected her with an auction house and she was back to work full-time.

Tomorrow

More networking, more contacts.
You think you've finished?

DAY 28

Good morning!

Today's Quote

The luckiest thing that happened to me is the fact that there was nobody who thought I would succeed.
—Arsenio Hall

Today's Focus

- You need to think how you are going to continue networking after you start your new job. Network within your new company, in social clubs, at political parties (see today's Helpful Hint), at associations. Once you isolate yourself, you are limiting your options.
- Continue your networking to find that new job. It's not in hand yet.
- A comparison chart can help you see which potential job best fits your needs.

Today's Helpful Hint

Get active politically. So many community needs, so many good contacts for now and the future.

Today's Goals

- Continue networking, interviewing, and going on second interviews. Also, keep adding to your list of Gatekeepers and contacts.
- Do a final organization of contacts for your permanent networking list.
- Form a ranking of job offers and interviews to come.

Today's Tasks

- Make your twenty calls and follow up.
- Go through your entire network list and pull out names for your permanent follow-up list.
- Continue to contact people on your permanent list—two or three per month, just to keep current.
- Double check that your job opportunities fit your dream. Review what your duties will be, who will be the boss, what kind of culture are you going into, and will you really be happy with the salary you will be making.

Today's Tickle

Go back to your Number-One Job Goal and make sure those criteria are still valid.

Today's Review

- Did you rank your offers? Did a clear winner emerge?
- Do you have your permanent networking list?

Today's Emotional Check

- What would you do if the offers are close and it's hard to decide? (See tomorrow.)
- Isn't this exciting?

Today's True Story

Julie was just out of graduate school. She wanted to find a job in her field. She used professors, colleagues, and friends. She used the Referent Power of older people and the alumni list from her school. A former professor was starting a company and needed an entry-level assistant. The professor knew Julie's work—because Julie kept in touch—and decided to make her an offer. He also hired three others in her class.

Tomorrow

Deciding tough choices on job offers.

DAY 29

Good morning!

Today's Quote

*How many a man has dated a new era in his life from
the reading of a book.*
—Henry David Thoreau

Today's Focus

- Making that final push by using networking.
- For those of you still bringing in offers, continue
  networking and following up.

Today's Helpful Hint

Often the decision you are looking for is within you and
it takes others to help you realize it.

Today's Goals

Network for help in decision making.

Today's Tasks

You have two offers. You gave them the same number of
points and you are not sure which to accept. How do you
decide?

Talk to five people in each organization:

- Your boss at each place
- Your boss's boss at each place

- Two people in the department where you will be working
- One person high up in another department

Ask them about your key concerns. Care must be taken not to reveal negatives about you, the job, the company, the working conditions. Let them know you are serious and that their offer is receiving strong consideration— that you are looking forward to working there. You can mention that you have another offer, but do not mention any details, such as who it's with or the salary level. They would not want you spreading details about the job they have offered you.

Today's Tickle

Go back and look at how your needs and your perception of what you want have changed. It's possible that you are being shaped by the opportunities in front of you. Step back and see if you can take a fresh look at the situation.

Today's Review

- What have you decided?
- What was the deciding factor? Future opportunities? Current working conditions?
- For those still working on contacts, aren't you much closer to a job than you were six weeks ago?

Today's Emotional Check

- Are you anticipating starting jitters?
- Are you happy with your choice?
- Are you going to continue to network? (You'd better!)

Today's True Story

Ken was a medical instrument technician. He had done his homework and learned, from an article in the paper, about a local company that was expanding into a new line of sophisticated instruments. Through a contact in his Bible study class, Ken found out that the individual interviewed in the newspaper article was quite approachable. So Ken did not ask for a job (he must have read this book!). He went in to discuss his ideas about the instruments mentioned in the article, and after ten minutes, he was offered a job!

Tomorrow

For those who are still looking, don't be discouraged.

DAY 30

Good morning!

Today's Quote

Tell the world!

Today's Focus

We need to address those of you who do not have an acceptable job offer yet. Don't give up. As we stated at the beginning of this book, there are factors beyond your control. They are not to be used as excuses to stop networking or to be used to make you feel it's futile. They are probably at the base of why you haven't been successful yet.

Do not give up networking. Do not give up contacting people. As always, see if you have areas of flexibility that can increase your areas of contacts. *But stay focused on your target*. Your best chance for a job is targeted networking. Do not let up until you have a job.

Today's Helpful Hint

Remember, the controls are in the hands of the Gatekeeper. The three major issues they will weigh are

- cost
- timing
- risk

The timing is probably the one that is frustrating you.

Today's Goals

Refocus and regain momentum, whether you are starting your new job or continuing your search.

Today's Tasks

- Continue networking, following up, and talking to Gatekeepers. If you think we're talking only to those who haven't found work, you're wrong! There's a Gatekeeper out there that has your *next* job. Get working!

Today's Tickle

Never forget what got you this job. Not just this book, not just support from people. It was *you* who did it.

Today's Review

You are now a consummate networker. Don't ever lose this skill. Use the network and your goals to drive you from here on out. You're in charge of your future (with a little help from your network).

Today's Emotional Check

Do not forget others! Never turn down a chance to help someone else. Remember how it felt when *you* needed help?

Today's True Story

Your story goes here.

Tomorrow

It's yours for the taking! Go get it!